Endorsements

Phill's book is conversational, easy to read, well thought out, highly personal, spiritual, and grace giving. He pierces the veneer of the traditional view of grace and helps the reader see the relational heart of grace. He pulls you into the heart of the Father, tearing down fear and shame, empowering the reader to take hold of the life we were made to live in Christ. There is much to consider here. I encourage you to read and contemplate.

—David Harwood,
Director of the Love of God Project.

Get ready for a deep-dive into the critical subject of grace! Phill guides us through history, theology, and life application, demonstrating that grace—the empowering presence of God with us—is more real, vibrant, and beautiful than we have realized. This book will challenge, inspire, provoke, and encourage you; all the while grounding you in this most critical element of the Christian faith. Phill has been deeply moved by God's grace, and through this book, you will too!

—Putty Putman,
School of Kingdom Ministry, Founder and Director

Once again, my prophetic friend Phill Urena has written a book that strengthens, encourages, and comforts. His fresh insights on grace will awaken your spirit and refresh your soul. Thank you, Phill, for the solid teaching within these pages.

—Dr. Ron Walborn,
VP & Dean of Nyack College and
Alliance Theological Seminary

Phill Urena's new book, *Redefining Grace*, tackles one of the meatiest problems in modern Protestant theology on a popular level. Historically, "grace" has carried the sense of kind, but undeserved, favor from God toward people. While this is somewhat true, it overlooks the understanding of the intimacy and power grace flows from. *Redefining Grace* unwraps the aspect of divinely given enablement to carry out that which God commands in a clear, powerful and deeply relational way. In this book, Phill teaches on enabling and empowering grace on a popular level, without the complex theological language that often confuses lay leaders. Importantly, he provides stories from his own life that illustrate that grace in action so the reader is encouraged and prompted to live in that grace as well. This book will spur you on toward courageous living with God, as you become His instrument in the world around you.

—Ken Fish,
Founder Orbis Ministries, Global Apostolic Minister

Because of the blood of Jesus Christ, we can truly live without condemnation, and without the fear of judgment or death. *Redefining Grace* is an encouraging journey; Phill Urena has researched the Scriptures and examined early church history to bring forward a practical and powerful understanding of this life-giving truth we call grace. *Redefining Grace* will bring freedom to those who have wrestled with condemnation, and move you to greater freedom and power to live the Christian life well.

Matt Bennett,
Founder and CEO of Christian Union

To
my friend
John, a true
prophet and man
of God,
keep doing what you're
doing. Love you Brother,
Phill

Redefining
grace

Redefining
grace
/grās/

verb

Living by His Presence
and Moving in His Power

PHILL URENA

DESTINY IMAGE® PUBLISHERS, INC.

P.O. Box 310, Shippensburg, PA 17257-0310

"Promoting Inspired Lives."

This book and all other Destiny Image and Destiny Image Fiction books are available at Christian bookstores and distributors worldwide.

Cover design by Eileen Rockwell

For more information on foreign distributors, call 717-532-3040.

Reach us on the Internet: www.destinyimage.com.

ISBN 13 TP: 978-0-7684-5450-5

ISBN 13 eBook: 978-0-7684-5451-2

ISBN 13 HC: 978-0-7684-5453-6

ISBN 13 LP: 978-0-7684-5452-9

For Worldwide Distribution, Printed in the U.S.A.

1 2 3 4 5 6 7 8 / 24 23 22 21 20

Dedication

TO MY AMAZING WIFE, PATTI. Your sacrifices to carry so much of the weight of family and finances, allowing me to pursue calling and destiny, is not lost on me; it is priceless and precious to me. Thank you doesn't begin to express enough. Nothing I do, nothing I was made for, could have happened without you. Thank you for allowing me to risk out countless times. When I failed, you stayed quiet and comforting. When I succeeded, you cheered me on. I am so glad we still have so much beauty in front of us. Forever! More than the stars!

Acknowledgments

TO MY GOOD FRIEND RACE ROBINSON, your incredibly valuable input in Biblical Hebrew and Greek, helped open up vision and understanding. I could never have tied together many of my thoughts and expressed them well without your direction and wisdom. You are truly an amazing man and dear friend. Thank you!

To Josh Hopping, for your theological input, historical insights, and thought-provoking input which helped keep me on track, not to mention your heartfelt encouragement. You drove this book home, thank you, you are a treasure. I see you!

To my dear friend Rip Wahlberg, our countless hours of conversation around this topic over the years, and your willingness to challenge me to do the work "that I might know," has brought a thoughtful, balanced perspective to the topic. It's also why it took this long, but also why it is what it is. This began in those hours and hours of discussion, so this is as much yours as it is mine. Love you, Bro!

Finally, Arthur Butts, my elder brother. You were the first to encourage me that I had the depth of biblical understanding to take this on. When I didn't believe in myself, you believed in me and my intellectual and theological capacity to take on the hard topics and to write this. I cherish all those late-night conversations in your dining room. Thanks for your encouragement and friendship. Forever young, Arthur.

Contents

Foreword

by Randy Clark

PHILL URENA'S *Redefining Grace: Living by His Presence and Moving in His Power* is a great new book on the subject of grace. Having read several books and many articles on grace, I found Phill's insights to be most encouraging. Phill writes with the heart of a spiritual father, and his experiences as a pastor make the book more enjoyable, enlightening, and energizing. I highly recommend the book, its illustrative stories, and its theological insights.

Redefining Grace resonated so powerfully with my understanding of grace. This understanding was influenced by some of the same fathers and doctors of the church. The insights from Irenaeus were significant. Like myself, Phill has drunk not only from the theological fountain of Western Christianity but also from the deep fountain of theological insight from Eastern Christianity. It was from the East that I learned the powerful understanding that the gifts of the Holy Spirit were not merely gifts but were the presence and power of the Holy Spirit. The gifts were the energies of God, and as such we were not just experiencing a gift of God; we were experiencing the very presence of God—His energies through which He makes Himself known to us. I have been looking for a book that expressed these insights regarding grace and gifts, or gracelets. A book that understood they were the ways an intimate God wants to manifest His very presence in us and through us.

I have been teaching at the Global Awakening Theological Seminary about the importance of understanding grace and gifts as experiencing the empowering presence of God through His energies. Phill has provided such a book. The Western Church, both Protestant and Roman Catholic, needs these insights.

Phill emphasizes that ultimately the gift of grace is Holy Spirit living in us. The sufficiency of grace is the life of the Spirit of God working in us, for us, and through us. His desire to take the theological idea of grace and bring us to a far more relationally intimate place, and from that understanding of grace take us to a far more powerful work (of grace—of God) in us and through us is powerful. Phill teaches us the grace of God brings life, light/truth, and the way of love from the inside out. His emphasis is not through a mechanism or power from God as much as the very life of God dwelling in us through the Spirit of love, light, and life lodging in the living-stones tabernacle.

Phill takes us on a journey through stories, literature—especially C.S. Lewis—word studies, theology, church history, and contemporary theological issues related to the place of grace in the life of the believer. He explains the Old Testament and New Testament concepts of grace and theology of grace; critically looks at the Augustinian and Calvinistic understanding of grace, bringing a more biblical balance; and spends several chapters on the relationship between the abundant life and grace. His unpacking of the importance of the energy of God in the life of Christ in us, which is the hope of glory, is one of the few places where I have found someone who is reading Paul as myself. I believe this understanding of grace as power or presence rather than undeserved favor or mercy is going to be much more commonly understood in the future than the present because this is a truth the Holy Spirit is bringing to the forefront of discipleship in the 21st century.

I loved the practical application of understanding grace as divine empowerment by the living Christ in us, by whose energy we labor so powerfully. I was especially intrigued to read the chapter that dealt with the tension between sovereignty and free will.

I hope the truths of this book create a better understanding of grace and gifts in the lives of its readers. I pray for you to purchase and read this fantastic book. I pray for you to experience Him in Holy Spirit, living by his energies—don't settle for a theology of grace that is more doctrinal than experiential. I pray for you to expect more and believe for more of Holy Spirit's revelations and power to flow through you, and that when this happens you will realize it isn't you who is the source of the revelation or the power, but the Tri-une God living in you via the Holy Spirit. Great job, Phill.

—Randy Clark, D.D., D.Min.
Author of *Destined for the Cross, Power to Heal, There Is More*
President of Global Awakening Theological Seminary
Overseer of the Apostolic Network of Global Awakening.

Introduction

Why Read This Book?

GRACE. I find this word fascinating as a descriptive of how God interacts with us.

Over the centuries, many have wrestled trying to understand what grace is. There are so many facets to grace, so many expressions of God's lovingkindness toward us—His children.

I remember, years ago, listening to a teaching by John Wimber on the gifts of the Spirit. He said the gifts are "gracelets," little demonstrations of God's favor and kindness toward us.

There are many ways God extends grace to us. Favor in a relationship, for example. When I think of my marriage, it is safe for me to say, if not for His kindness, mercy, and presence, we may not have made it through all that life has thrown at us. I am happily, faithfully, and joyfully married because of His grace. Oh, the countless expressions of God's grace-filled life in us and for us.

This book is not about His graciousness, the kindness He gives to us moment by moment throughout our life. My dad would say to me, "Remember when you want to judge others, you don't know the shoes they have walked in, their pain and struggles. Also, remember, there but by the grace of God go I." He was acutely aware it was God's kindness toward him that he was even alive, married, and had a family. These expressions of God's grace are not what I am writing about, though I value all His kindnesses toward us.

It is important to understand that God interacts with us in an empowering way. It comes in different expressions, based on our need in the moment, what He is working into us, the season we are in, the state of our heart, and our connection with Him, just to name a few. His grace is the power that draws us, the power that keeps us, the power that transforms us and more.

My big question is, what *is* that power? While this will not be an exhaustive study on biblical grace, I am writing this book with the hope that, as you read, your perspective of grace would shift in such a way as to draw you closer to Him—that you may discover greater joy and greater freedom. My desire is to draw you deeper into the revelation of God's amazing love; to draw you more fully into His amazing grace and perhaps cause a shift in your perspective, understanding, and application of what grace is.

My journey with the Lord is saturated with His generosity, kindness, and power through Holy Spirit. Unexpected miracles and signs that made me wonder. It has been a journey, an adventure, really, of both self-discovery and God discovery. The God discovery part has been way better than the self-discovery part. However, you can't have God discovery and not also have what it reveals about yourself. It is the trade-off to know Him intimately; it is worth it. I hope as you read through these pages a shift happens that brings greater freedom, deeper love, and a greater expression of His grace in your life.

What I hope to share is an understanding of grace seldom expressed, taught, or understood. Grace is more than an undeserved gift of God. In fact, that is a deficient definition of His grace. I believe, for the redeemed, grace is the life of Holy Spirit in us, flowing out from us and for us, as we say, "Yes, Lord."

As you read through this book, I hope you will have revelation after revelation, discovering a deeper understanding of God—Father, Son, and Holy Spirit. May you discover the awe of His purposes. May you fall deeper in love with your Father, your Lord, and the Spirit of God living in you.

> Lord, would You cause the words of this book to ignite a fire in Your children. As they read, draw them into a greater revelation of You and who they are in You. I pray they would find "gracelets" as they move forward, intimate gems between You and them, causing their hearts to see You more clearly. May they be transformed, becoming more like You, and may they love

more fiercely just like You do. In the end, Lord, would You empower them to make You known, vessels of Your amazing grace, with boldness and fearlessness, going after Your Kingdom and making You known with both words and the demonstration of the Spirit's power, in the name of Jesus! Amen!

Chapter 1

Understanding the Theology of Grace

The notion of God's love coming to us free of charge, no strings attached, seems to go against every instinct of humanity. The Buddhist eight-fold path, the Hindu doctrine of karma, the Jewish covenant, and the Muslim code of law—each of these offers a way to earn approval. Only Christianity dares to make God's love unconditional.

—C.S. Lewis

My Grace Journey—Part One

ON DECEMBER 19, 1982, I had an encounter with the power of grace. It came at an unlikely place and an unlikely time. I was introduced to my best friend, Jesus, and that day I was forever ruined for any other. Oddly enough, my encounter with Him was not what you might expect. Eight months earlier I was on my face crying out to God, hopeless, afraid, and empty. Every part of my life was under siege. I was only 27 years old and felt hopeless and alone.

I owned a small company that sold rare coins to investors when I discovered my partners were stealing behind my back. At the same time, my brother-in-law, who was my assistant manager, was falsely accusing me of wrongdoing to my sales team, many of whom were good friends. He was maligning my character with no cause and no truth. In addition to this, my wife, Patti, and I were struggling relationally over the combination of poor finances and her infertility.

I knew I was going to lose my business, friendships, and possibly my home. I was okay with all of that, I can rebuild those things—but I wasn't willing to lose my wife. One day, in the midst of this hopelessness, as I was pacing in my home office, wearing down my carpet, I fell on my knees and wept. I cried out to the Jesus of my childhood and said, "God, I feel like I am going to die, I am losing everything. If You are real, will You rescue me from this place? I will serve You for the rest of my life."

As I was weeping, I felt anxiety release me and peace come upon me. I wish I could say my life miraculously changed for the better at that moment; I cannot. In fact, nothing changed significantly or even measurably. I was still living a sinner's life. Patti and I were still struggling, it even got worse for a while.

I still felt lost and circumstances remained unchanged. I still had tremendous anxiety; fear filled me. A few weeks later, I received a phone call from a guy who used to work with me, Craig. He said, "I want to share a business opportunity with you, can I come over?" Well, the short story is, I joined Amway, a popular networking marketing business at that time. Hook, line, and sinker, I jumped in. I just wanted to dig out of this financial hole we were in and I was willing to do anything to do it. I wanted to prove to Patti that I wasn't a loser, that she didn't make a mistake marrying me. The Lord was in this, though I had no clue at the time. My motives were not godly, they were survival.

Within the Amway organization, there was an amazing couple in their early 40s, Frank and Donna. They were in our "upline." They were relatively successful in Amway, and they were humble and authentic Jesus followers. They were fun to be with and very caring. Compared to the many "holy rollers" we had met, they were incredibly safe. In fact, in my walk with the Lord I have met few safer. By that I mean they seemed more interested in Patti and I than in the money we could make them, and that drew us in. They too had struggled with infertility and had plenty of compassion for us. Donna loved on Patti so well. They never preached at us, they just loved us.

About seven months into our Amway life, we went to one of three or four major conferences held each year. I believe it was called "Dream Weekend." Little did I know my prayer from so many months earlier, which I had completely forgotten, was about to be fulfilled. For no discernable reason, the whole weekend I kept thinking, *My life is going to completely change this weekend.* I thought I was going to get the key to success and everything would come together for me. I would show Patti I could be a success and not the failure I felt I was. I would prove myself to her, be her knight in shining armor, her dream come true.

Time was running out, though. It was Saturday, the big night, the last chance for me to get that key, the one that would turn everything around, save our home and our marriage. It was a great evening, real motivational stuff, but no answers, no key to success I could grab hold of.

Before the night session began, Frank and Donna had invited us to join them at a nondenominational Sunday service that Amway had at all their weekend conferences. Many of Amway's leaders, at least in this organization, were believers in those days. We decided to go, mostly because we loved Frank and Donna, but for me also because the speaker was a guy named Paul Miller.

Paul Miller was the starting quarterback at the University of North Carolina from 1969 through 1971. As a teen-crazed football fan, I would watch him on TV late Saturday afternoons after my high school games. He was one of my favorite college players. If he was going to speak, I would be there. So, we got up early, got ready, and went to hear Paul Miller. Our friends saved us great seats, second row from the front, first two seats on the aisle. These were the seats you'd pay big bucks for at a concert, sporting event, or

Broadway show. This was going to be great, just 40 feet from Paul Miller. Maybe I could even meet him and get an autograph. I didn't realize we were being set up for easy access when the time came.

Paul shared his story. How he was always "the guy" because of his athleticism. In high school he led his football, basketball, and baseball teams to state championships. In college, he was an All-ACC quarterback and the ACC Brian Piccolo Award winner. I was soaking it all in. But then he shared his life after college, how he struggled in several areas, including his marriage. He told us how desperate he became and how he came to Jesus.

As he arrived at the climax of his testimony, tears rolled down his face, and I was drawn in. I could relate so much to his story. I was feeling emotional, too, but didn't understand why. Did I feel for him, or was this about me? I couldn't be sure. I just sat there looking at Paul Miller, star athlete, failed, almost lost his marriage, how is that possible? This guy I looked up to some twelve years earlier, had been as broken as me.

After a time, he invited the worship team up to the stage. They played "Amazing Grace" and Paul invited any who wanted to give their lives to Jesus to come forward. I didn't exactly know what that meant, but I knew I needed to respond. Weeping, both Patti and I went up. I think she went up more for me than for herself, but the Lord honored us both. I don't even remember walking. I think I may have been translated to the front, like Philip in the Book of Acts.

I don't know what happened, all I know is I found myself at the front of the stage weeping and praying along with my hero Paul Miller.

I was sobbing so deeply, like I'd never wept before, as waves of liquid love washed over me again and again and again. I don't know if that moment was five minutes or an hour long. That day amazing grace filled me, poured over me, saturated me. That encounter wrecked me for any other love. Grace, this amazing grace, drew me deep into His love and I would never be the same. I had found the key to everything—and I was indeed changed forever. That song, as old as it is, no matter how many times I hear it, brings me back to that moment and to tears. *"Amazing grace, how sweet the sound that saved a wretch like me...."* Grace, what a gift. Grace, what a powerful gift from God it is.

In that moment and in my early walk with Jesus, I had no concept of a theology of grace. It was simply God touching this lost sinner, giving me life, and bringing me into His embrace. I was forgiven. Overwhelming hopelessness was overtaken by overcoming hopefulness in His undying love and devotion to me, personally.

He was living in me, and whatever that meant was enough for me. I was invaded by the God who is love. I was alive in ways I could only dream of. The honeymoon wouldn't last forever, there would be work to do, battles to be won; in time the grace-birthed and grace-sustained transformation would come. In that moment, and the short months following, I was "in love" with Him, my wife, everyone. The light of His beautiful love was turned on and thankfully, it has never left me.

The enemy has tempted me to question God's love and my sonship. My own sin has at times tried to overshadow His life and love in me. But as long as I turn my face toward Him, He brings me through. What you set your eyes on, you attract. I've learned to fix my eyes on Him in all situations, and His grace is enough.

Grace: The Church's General Perspective

It is important to unwrap the different theological views of grace, how they formed the way we see our relationship with God and His with us. We will walk through a bit of the history of the theology and teachings on grace, so we can understand the process and how the Church landed on certain points. Note: for this discussion, the term "Church" means the universal Church of all believers in the Lord Jesus Christ.

This unwrapping is important because many believers have been taught positions and have owned and even defended positions without knowing why or how the theological positions and beliefs came to be. I want to take you on a journey, and I encourage you to come with me. It may seem tedious and too theological at times, but it will be worth it once we land. So please don't jump over this chapter; if you stick with me as we move forward, you will understand in a more personally intimate way the beauty of our God and His heart for you. The mystery will be revealed.

Grace—what an interesting term. The Church has been wrestling with it for ages. What is grace? As I have contemplated and wrestled with that question for nearly four decades, I have come to realize it is so much more than we make it to be; and at the same time, it is everything we have made it to be and yet simpler and more relational. The idea that grace is defined primarily as "God's unmerited favor" doesn't capture how it empowers dramatic transformation and releases so much power in and through the life of a child of God.

Let's take a moment and look at this word that is so important to our faith. In the Greek language, the word *grace* is *charis;* from which *charisma* is derived. *Charis* is a secular Greek word that the apostles chose to use for a spiritual purpose. Generally, it means a kindness given, favor bestowed, a gift. It is a term often used for when someone of greater stature is generous toward a lesser by offering them a kindness, a gift of favor.[1]

Charis most often was used for artistic or poetic purpose. For instance, when we see a bride in her dress we might say, "You look radiant," or, "She carries such grace." We are being poetic; we are making an aesthetic statement. However, *charis* also had a lesser used ethical meaning as well. If we were left with no more understanding than this, it would seem an odd word to explain God's grace. However, there was more to this word as it began to be used in a different context; one of power.

> It may be added that in later Greek *'charis'* also had the sense of force or *power*. It could be a spell, or demonic force, affecting human life with supernatural influences. In Euripides, it was a power from the underworld that could convey the virtues of a dead hero to his living family or followers. This sense, too, though set in a new context, was used in the New Testament: grace became the power of God to enable Christians to live the new life in Christ.[2]

Looking at the two expressions of grace mentioned—"saving grace" and "empowering grace" and only these two expressions—it is important to understand that the apostles were looking for language to communicate something beyond prior human experience. When you are speaking of the Maker of all things, words are naturally limited in capturing fully who He is or what He is doing.

Finding the right words can be challenging at the least and often not perfect. They were choosing the best words available to help people understand how the Spirit engages humans at salvation and the power given moment by moment as we walk out the personal process of transformation. It is not something simply given at the moment of salvation, it is to be lived from moment by moment, throughout our lives.

There are many Scriptures that support the thought that the power of God is what sustains us, keeps us, and empowers us to be exactly what He created us to be—sons and daughters who overcome darkness and shine with His light. Perhaps Second Corinthians 12:9 is the best-known verse, *"But he said to me, 'My grace is sufficient for you, for my power is made perfect in weakness'"* (2 Corinthians 12:9). We can see in this verse that there is an ongoing relationship between God's grace and our capacity to live a Spirit-empowered life. There are many other verses in Scripture to support this understanding of grace. The following are just a few:

> *He gives power to the faint, and to him who has no might he increases strength* (Isaiah 40:29).

> *I can do all things through him who strengthens me* (Philippians 4:13).

> *For I, the Lord your God, hold your right hand; it is I who say to you, "Fear not, I am the one who helps you"* (Isaiah 41:13).

> *...but with the temptation he will also provide the way of escape, that you may be able to endure it* (1 Corinthians 10:13).

The idea is this, we are not just *saved* by grace—we are *sustained, empowered, and live* by grace. This is a strong biblical theme. The Lord is intimately connected with His children. However, He doesn't control us. We can choose to sustain ourselves through our own power, this is essentially what happened in the Garden of Eden, which led to the sin nature. Or we can choose to live a surrendered, life-giving relationship through Christ, actively receiving grace throughout our day-to-day living.

Every day, in all circumstances, we can still choose which tree we will eat from. If we eat from the Tree of the Knowledge of Good and Evil, we are choosing to say, "I got this, God...no need to help." If we eat from the Bread of Life, The Tree of Life, we are choosing to say, "With Your grace, God, I receive Your help." His power allows us to live and walk through the circumstances of life in victory.

As noted previously, our English word *charisma* comes from the Greek word root *charis*. According to the Oxford Dictionary, charisma means, "to possess compelling attractiveness or charm that can inspire devotion in others. A divinely conferred power or talent." It is to possess the gift or talent to influence people; it is "power to influence." It is not passive, it is active.

When we talk of biblical grace, we need to remember it is a gift of God, it has purpose and is powerful. We can't stir it up or make it happen; it is God initiated. God is working His influence into our lives, not through control but through loving relationship. There is no doubt about it, He is at work in us all the time. Grace is an inward working that transforms us into the fullness of Christ. Outwardly grace brings forth His image to make Him known through our lives.

In the hands of an unscrupulous master, this can be scary, and deadly. Think of men like Jim Jones, founder of the Peoples Temple cult that climaxed with mass sui-cides in Jonestown, Guyana. Or David Koresh and the Branch Davidians. Or a more familiar name today, David Miscavige the leader of Scientology. All these men had or have charisma, the power to influence, to charm and cast a spell on people to follow their sinister agenda and belief systems.

God, on the other hand, is faithful, kind, and perfect in love, wholly trustworthy. He doesn't force His will on us; He draws us near, by grace, into greater revelations of His love.

Seeing grace as power to influence would have been part of how those living in the first-century Greco-Roman world would have applied *charis*. It would be part of the secularization of *charis*. An almost divine power to influence people. Peter, John, and Paul understood this application and used it to describe God's working in people to bring them into the saving work of Jesus on the Cross.

In summary, the writers of the New Testament were look-ing for words to describe and instruct this new revelation in Jesus. They naturally, just as we would today, would have sought after language that common people would under-stand to help them take hold of the gift of life provided through Christ Jesus. In our modern English, it doesn't quite translate the same, but it is no less valuable. *Charis* has differ-ent applications within different contexts; for us, the context is one of God's love and kindness.

Types of Grace

The theological definition of grace as "God's unmerited favor" is problematic for me. Not because it is possible to earn salvation by works, you cannot. I agree with Paul in Ephesians 2:8-9. Our works are dirty rags compared to His gift of life (see Isaiah 64:6). It isn't that I disagree; but I ask, when is any gift of love earned?

What does it mean to say grace is God's unmerited favor? This issue of unmerited favor, undeserved or unearned favor, comes up against what love is. A gift of love is never about deserving or merit, it is freely given or it isn't love. I am fully aware and agree we were all sinners, and as sinners the gift of life through the Cross is undeserved. His saving grace invaded our being the moment we said, "Forgive me for my sins."

What I have seen, however, is that all too often, the focus is on our unworthiness—not on His amazing love or on His high value for His children. If the value of something is based on the price someone is willing to pay, God said we are incredibly valuable to Him. And while by our standards we feel unworthy, by His standards and by the price Jesus paid on the Cross, we are worthy of His salvation—though we don't deserve it. This is one theme of this book that we will walk through together.

A gift of love doesn't consider merit; giving something on merit is a wage or a payment for something. On Christmas or a birthday, we don't stop and say to ourselves, "Does my child deserve a present for Christmas or their birthday?" And we don't say to them on those days, "Here is your gift, you don't deserve it, but I am giving it you anyway." No, love is always free. True love, unconditional love, is never something we give in reciprocation for being loved. If it isn't "freely" given, it isn't love.

God cherishes humankind so highly that He gave His Son once for all. In the parables of The Pearl of Great Price (Matthew 13:45-46) and The Lost Sheep (Luke 15:1-6), we can see just what He is willing to do to pursue us. He determines our worth; we may not deserve Him by our actions, but that doesn't define our value or worth to Him.

To bring you on this journey of redefining our understanding of grace, I need to give some historical background for the theological positions foundational to the Church's teaching on salvation, original sin, predestination, and freewill. There is more to understanding grace than a simple "we are saved by grace." I will provide a brief, hopefully clear summary of how the Church's understanding of grace impacts our beliefs. Our beliefs are what cause us to behave as we do.

Historically, there have been two general theological schools of thought. Calvinism, which says everything is predestined as God wills, especially who gets saved. The other is Arminianism, which stands on people's freewill to choose God or reject Him. Most Christians attend church denominations that fall into the teachings of John Calvin or Jacobus Arminius or have been influenced by their teaching. There are other theological views, but to look at them all would be too exhaustive for the purpose of this book. For our purposes, we will focus on these two as they have been the most influential over the past 500 years.

What Is Common Grace?

Before we look at the expressions of grace that are our main discussion points, it may be helpful to look briefly at "common grace," which God provides for everyone on planet Earth. Jesus best describes common grace in Matthew 5:

> *You have heard that it was said, "You shall love your neighbor and hate your enemy." But I say to you, Love your enemies and pray for those who persecute you, so that you may be sons of your Father who is in heaven. **For he makes his sun rise on the evil and on the good and sends rain on the just and on the unjust.** For if you love those who love you, what reward do you have? Do not even the tax collectors do the same? And if you greet only your brothers, what more are you doing than others? Do not even the Gentiles do the same? You therefore must be perfect, as your heavenly Father is perfect* (Matthew 5:43-48).

Jesus is telling us that God provides what we need whether you are good or evil, righteous or unrighteous. He goes on to say that we are to do the same, we are called to love like our Father, *"You therefore must be perfect, as your heavenly Father is perfect."* Perfect means mature, complete; exactly as you are made to be. In this case the focus is unconditional love and kindness toward others, the deserving and the undeserving.

Therefore, common grace is the basis God provides in order for all people to live. Whether you believe in God—Father, Jesus, and Holy Spirit—or not, you live only by His kindness to provide the means for life. Everyone has common grace; what we do with it is something else. My personal belief is that common grace is sufficient to believe that there is a God and to make moral choices.

> *For since the creation of the world God's invisible qualities–his eternal power and divine nature–have been clearly seen, being understood from what has been made, so that people are without excuse* (Romans 1:20 NIV).

What Is Saving Grace?

The historically accepted definition for *saving grace* has been God's "unmerited favor," we see this in Catholicism, Calvinism, and Arminianism. The Merriam-Webster Dictionary and the Oxford Dictionary define grace as *unmerited divine assistance or favor*. A simple online search will support this definition of grace. There are those today arguing against this understanding of grace. To expand on it would be to define it as underserved and unearned gift from God for salvation. The unmerited redemptive power of God for those who believe.

Saint Augustine was a fourth-century theologian and the Bishop of Hippo. In his writing *On Grace and Free Will,* he writes in Chapter 7 (emphasis mine):

> Therefore, my dearly beloved, as we have now proved by our former testimonies from Holy Scripture that *there is in man a free determination of will for living rightly and acting rightly; so now let us see what are the divine testimonies concerning the grace of God, without which we are not able to do any good thing.* And first of all, I will say something about the very profession which you make in your brotherhood.

Augustine starts with supporting freewill, and then goes on to say, "The grace of God, without which we are not able to do *any good things."* Later in Chapter 13, he states:

> From these and similar passages of Scripture, we gather the proof that *God's grace is not given according to our merits.* The truth is, we see that it is given not only where there are no good, but even where there are many evil merits preceding: and we see it so given daily. But it is plain that when

> it has been given, also our good merits begin to
> be—yet only by means of it; for, were that only
> to withdraw itself, man falls, not raised up, but
> precipitated by free will.

It is important to note that Augustine is not defining grace as unmerited favor, but rather he is sharing on the nature of grace; it's not given based on merit. This may seem like semantics, but the subtlety is not insignificant. He is focused on the truth that grace is a gift, and gifts are not given because of merit. It is given freely and not in response to something.

To say it is unmerited favor is to place the focus on our unworthiness rather than God's lovingkindness. Somehow, from Augustine's teaching on the way grace and freewill operate together in our walk with God, we go from supporting "God's gift can't be earned," to the place we find much of the church from the Reformation on—we are wretched sinners who do not deserve anything good from God.

The grace narrative in Scripture is integral, not just to our salvation, but our entire walk and relationship with God. It is not open to debate; we have been saved by grace, the gift of life given by a loving Father through the compassionate, selfless sacrifice of His Son, Jesus. It is a living grace that continues to keep us by the Spirit alive in us.

> *But God, being rich in mercy,* **because of the great**
> **love with which he loved us, even when we**

> *were dead in our trespasses, made us alive*
> *together with Christ—by grace you have been*
> *saved—and raised us up with him and seated us with*
> *him in the heavenly places in Christ Jesus, so that in the*
> *coming ages he might show the immeasurable riches of*
> *his grace in kindness toward us in Christ Jesus. For by*
> *grace you have been saved through faith. And*
> *this is not your own doing; it is the gift of God,*
> *not a result of works, so that no one may boast*
> (Ephesians 2:4-9).

While grace is foundational to our faith, in its expressions as saving grace and empowering grace, I don't agree with the emphasis of unmerited favor. I say this because I don't see where *charis* actually means unmerited favor. I am not convinced because I have not found the word *unmerited* in any Greek dictionary, concordance, or lexicon. I also have not found the word *unmerited* to describe *chen,* the Hebrew word translated grace. What I have found in Strong's Concordance, Thayer's Lexicon, and other sources is that both *charis* and *chen* are given the same meanings. I like this following description or definition:

> Grace - that which affords joy, pleasure, delight, sweetness, charm, loveliness: grace of speech, good will, loving-kindness; the favor of the merciful kindness by which *God, exerting his holy influence upon souls,* turns them to Christ, keeps, strengthens, increases them in Christian faith,

43

> knowledge, affection, and kindles them to the
> exercise of the Christian virtues.[3]

Notice that nowhere in this definition is the word *unmerited*. While it does mean favor, kindness, to be looked upon favorably, it also exerts power to move humankind toward God. But unmerited is not part of the equation; that doesn't diminish the gift of grace. In fact, it makes it more beautiful. Just as the Father initiated the New Covenant by sending His only begotten Son to die on the Cross. The death and resurrection of Jesus made available saving grace to humankind.

Humans did not initiate the means to salvation, the Living God did. He did it because, *"God so **loved** the world He gave His only begotten Son"* (John 3:16). It was His love, and merit has nothing to do with it. Grace is His provision that we may be born-again children of God by His Spirit—and it comes solely from His great love.

We are going to spend considerable time looking at this issue; but for now let's agree that merited or unmerited should not be part of the grace equation.

Calvin and Grace

Church denominations that associate doctrines with the reformer John Calvin are Calvinists and subscribe to Calvinism. In North America, the denominations that fall under this category are the Reformed Baptists, the Presbyterian Church (USA and Canada), many Anglican churches, the Congregational Church, the Dutch Reformed Church, and several others. There are also some charismatics that follow Reformed Theology, or Calvinism, though most generally do not.

I have some dear charismatic friends who are counted among those who are Calvinists. They are amazing leaders and among the brightest, most loving and generous people and leaders I know. While we do not agree on certain points, I value their wisdom, authenticity, love, and friendship. We can disagree on theological points and still be loving, supportive brothers and sisters.

Five key points to Calvinism and Reformed Theology are expressed with the acronym TULIP. The first is, **T**otal depravity, which we will examine in more detail. Point two is **U**nconditional election, which simply means there is nothing humans can do to move God to choose us. Either we are chosen or not. Then **L**imited atonement and **I**rresistible grace, we will examine these as well. Finally, **P**reservation of the saints, which says, "Once saved, always saved."

Let's first look at the theological position of "total depravity." How you see this issue is tied into how you define "original sin." The second-century church father Irenaeus was the first who wrote on original sin, seeing it very different from Calvin. We will look at his view in the next chapter on original sin.

Saint Augustine's writings were more influential on the Church's teachings on original sin. Augustine was a student of Greek philosophy before becoming a Christian. He had a brilliant mind and applied philosophical reasoning to his understanding of Scripture teachings. There is much to Augustine's writings that are beneficial. He wrote and established his view of "original sin" in response to a fourth-century heresy called Pelagianism.

According to Merriam-Webster dictionary, Pelagianism is *"one agreeing with Pelagius in denying original sin and consequently in holding that individuals have perfect freedom to do either right or wrong."* Pelagius taught original sin did not taint human nature and "mortal will" is capable of choosing good or evil without any special divine aid. Augustine taught that original sin is the release of the sin nature in humankind through Adam to all his descendants through the generations. One of the by-products of this perspective tainted the Church's view on sex, even marital sex, as original sin was directly passed down seed by seed through sexual intimacy generationally, according to Augustine.

We are not contesting that sin entered the world through the one man, Adam. Certainly the Bible supports this view, not the least of which would be Romans 5:12 (NIV), *"Therefore, just as sin entered the world through one man, and death through sin, and in this way death came to all people, because all sinned."*

Before the Reformation, Christianity in the West was primarily informed by Roman Catholicism (today's western European countries). The Eastern Church (including today's Middle East, Asia Minor, Eastern Europe, etc.) did not hold to Augustine's teachings on total depravity, original sin, or the theological concept that God alone regenerates. The Eastern view was that both God and humankind are engaged in the salvation process. The East-West schism was something that gradually happened over many hundreds of years. As early as AD 180, there was rising division within various regions with the Roman Church's claim to have greater authority through the papacy.

The idea that popes have a special position as those in authoritative descendancy due to both Peter and Paul being martyred in Rome became a point of contention between the churches of the East and West. Due to the separation of the Church into the Eastern Church and the Western Church in 1054, it is understandable that Augustine and other Catholic scholars would have great influence on the European churches and the Theology of the Reformation. However, Calvin and Augustine, while they agreed with salvation by grace, their view of it is quite different. Calvin went further in his application of original sin and in his application of grace, as well.

In his article for *The Evangelical Quarterly* titled "The Doctrine of Grace in Calvin and Augustine," Dr. Larry D. Sharp states:

> Calvin followed Augustine in affirming the heart of the doctrine of original sin: that Adam's death in sin meant the death in sin of us all and that this

state is passed down to all persons, even newborn infants. But for Calvin the essence of this sin is not mere self-love as in Augustine, but pride and rebellion and outright disobedience. Original sin is not merely a privation or an emptiness of original righteousness, but rather a blatant perversity which is always actively producing the works of the flesh.

The effect of Adam's sin is not only a wound and a sickness, as in Augustine, but is a total depravity and corruption. To describe sin as a lack of health and light and righteousness is to Calvin not to have "expressed effectively enough its power and energy." The result of Adam's sin is more properly called the *ruin* of man than the *illness* of man.[4]

Dr. Sharp goes on to say, regarding Augustine's view of grace:

In the Anti-Pelagian writings Augustine does not give us a single definition of grace. As he most often uses the term it refers to God's healing power and is closely associated with the Holy Spirit and with God's poured-out love.[5]

We can see from the time of Calvin the idea of the sinfulness of humanity went to a place it had not gone before.

Yes, our flesh wrestles with inclinations toward sin; however, Paul gives us room to access the overcoming power of Christ in Romans 8 and other places, as well. Calvin takes us to an almost hopeless place and perhaps, not intentionally, to a works mentality. This leaves many believers in a heightened place of religiosity, shame, and hopelessness to ever find true victory. They believe that they are incapable of goodness, it is our fallen nature to sin, to sin compulsively and continually. And though by the Spirit we can overcome, many, as they fail and continue to strive to do better, become hopeless and some even give up. However, the very resting in God's goodness the Scripture exhorts us to, is to rest in His love for us and His work in us. The writer of Hebrews 4:1-3 (NIV) speaks into this when he writes:

> *Therefore, since* **the promise of entering his rest still stands, let us be careful that none of you be found to have fallen short of it.** *For we also have had the good news proclaimed to us, just as they did; but the message* **they heard was of no value to them, because they did not share the faith of those who obeyed.** *Now we who have believed enter that rest....*

They didn't share in His rest because they could not obey in faith or take hold of the promises faithfully. What is the promise? There are many, but for our conversation, I would point to God is good, God is love, God is faithful to the humble that call out to Him and trust in His unfailing love. We don't live in right relationship with Him by anything more than our faith in His faithfulness toward us, and the humility to surrender our hearts, wills, and lives in love and worship.

The next point is whether predestination is for an elect group of people, what Calvin called limited atonement along with what he called irresistible grace, or invincible grace. Calvin taught that God chose beforehand those people who would be saved, the elect, all others have been chosen for destruction, there is nothing anyone can do about it. Due to total depravity, man did not have the capacity of freewill, beyond simple life choices. Hence, man did not possess the spiritual capacity of freewill needed to choose salvation. We are incapable to choose between Jesus and life, Heaven, or hell. If God has not chosen us, we are lost without hope. Those that were already determined by God to be saved, those marked for limited atonement, would receive irresistible grace at just the right moment. Irresistible grace is God's gift to the pre-chosen elect; they cannot resist it. The elect also do nothing to lose it, it is invincible. For those pre-chosen, grace is irresistible and invincible, choice is removed. In a nutshell, God gives the elect a type of grace, irresistible grace, that empowers the individual to accept "saving grace" at the correct time. At the point of salvation grace becomes invincible and you cannot choose to walk away from God.

You cannot lose your salvation. Why is this truth important to understand? Because with the Reformation, the Doctrine of Irresistible Grace became a deeply rooted core value for many Christians, and it still is today. This position is foundational to Calvinism and Reformed Theology. The idea that a person cannot choose Jesus apart from God first choosing the individual means we have no choice in our salvation. If we lean into this theological view, it impacts our definition and understanding of grace in very specific ways. Not the least of which is, you cannot resist God, so you cannot turn away from Him and lose your salvation.

I personally find this view is not strongly supported in Scripture or in the early Church. Some have tried to use some of the following statement by early Church fathers to support the sovereignty of God, in terms of man having limited freewill. They say this is the substructure or foundation for unconditional election and irresistible grace. I would beg to differ. I see the freewill to respond in these statements. You be your own judge.

> Let us review all the generations in turn and learn that from generation to generation *the Master has given an opportunity for repentance to those who desire to turn* to him (1 Clement 7.5).
>
> So then, having already planned everything in his mind together with his Child, he permitted us during the former time to be carried away by undisciplined impulses as we desired, led astray by pleasures and lusts, not at all because he took delight in our sins, but because he was patient; not because he approved of that former season

> of unrighteousness, but because he was creating the present season of righteousness, in order that we who in the former time were convicted by our own deeds as unworthy and, having clearly demonstrated *our inability to enter the kingdom of God on our own, might be enabled to do so by God's power* (The Epistle to Diognetus).

Some have reasoned that these statements from the early Church fathers support unconditional election. I disagree. Clement's statement clearly points to "given an opportunity" to repent. How do you separate choice from opportunity? An opportunity is an invitation requiring a response. You might say, "Well it is semantics, God still causes the person to make the choice God wants." If that is the case, opportunity is a very bad choice of words.

In the second, Clement speaks into the truth that we can't enter the Kingdom without Christ; he isn't saying some are predetermined to get in and others are not. These are convenient stretches. Am I saying God is not sovereign? Absolutely not, He is Lord of all. I am simply saying that He can be in control and not be controlling. His sovereignty includes our freewill. He knows our choices and He knows His desires; He knows how to train up His children. He wants lovers, true love never comes from being controlled.

As my children grew, they had more freedom to make choices. There were times I knew they were going to make choices that would bring painful experiences. I didn't take the choices away; if I did, how could I prepare them to make good choices. When we remove choice, we empower codependency. Instead, I would help them process their thoughts and emotions before making their choice. I did this at times knowing they were still going to choose the wrong road. Was I still their dad? Yes. Where they living under my roof on my dime? Absolutely. Could I have forbidden those poor choices that would lead to hurt? Yes. Did it seem sometimes I should have, that it may have been more loving? Yes, perhaps. Perhaps in the moment that would have been more protective, and it may seem more loving. It also may have short-circuited their maturing process. We learn so much from choices gone wrong, and how we process the ramification of those choices.

However, my goal was never to simply raise my sons to make good choices today by taking freedom from them. The goal was to help them gain wisdom, to live well for the rest of their lives, and to empower them to grow in true wisdom. I often tell parents, "You are raising your children with the goal that at 25 they will have the wisdom and understanding to make good life choices."

Did I have full control over my sons? No, and at times I really wish I did, it would have been easier. But did I have some influence to guide them and the confidence they would get there in time? Absolutely.

Why did God make us? Was it simply to have a species of beings that would serve Him and worship obediently? That is how the ancients understood their false gods. Man existed to serve at the whim of those greater than them. There was no love, it was fear. Our God, the Trinity, made us for the most intimate fellowship. Our service is not from fear but a loving response to His great love. God made us for relationship with Him. Relationship without choice is slavery, not sonship. Relationship without the freedom to choose, even choose badly, is not love, it is control.

Arminius and Grace

Now enter Jacob Arminius, a Dutch Reformed pastor and theologian. He was a student of John Calvin's hand-picked replacement Theodore Beza. Arminius, while he did agree with total depravity, he did not agree with irresistible grace or with limited atonement. Arminius thought that man had the capacity to make moral choices, whether through an awareness of God by what could be seen of Him in creation or through gained moral wisdom. For Arminius, freewill was essential. Christ paid for the sins of all humankind—unlimited atonement.

While he also taught we were saved by grace alone, just as Calvin did, but not by irresistible grace, Arminius taught prevenient grace or preceding grace. The thought was that God released into people's lives a preceding grace, you might call it an empowered invitation, it could be acted upon or resisted. In his mind, prevenient grace preserved the freewill we were given to choose saving grace or to resist God.

He also believed we could resist Holy Spirit in the walking out our faith life, meaning it was possible to walk away from God and lose salvation. Without saving grace, man is lost; and without the Spirit-initiating grace in an unbeliever, they would not be saved—but by the person's will, a choice is made.

> *For the grace of God has appeared that offers salvation to **all** people. It teaches us to say "No" to ungodliness and worldly passions, and to live self-controlled, upright and godly lives in this present age, while we wait for the blessed hope–the appearing of the glory of our great God and Savior, Jesus Christ, who gave himself for us to redeem us from all wickedness and to purify for himself a people that are his very own, eager to do what is good* (Titus 2:11-14 NIV).

What we can agree with is grace comes from God. We can also agree it is not earned, it is a gift; the nature of a gift is something given freely. Is it possible we have emphasized the wrong understanding of the definition of *charis?* The word *charis*, like so many other Greek words, has many varied applications. Words in the English language are more well defined than many ancient Greek words. In Greek, context has to be considered, as does the purpose of the speaker. If we consider the understanding of this word as, at least in part, the power to influence, it may better serve us.

The Arminian Response:
Preceding Grace

There is a potential problem in the idea of prevenient grace, also known as preceding or anticipatory grace. It is a grace given to all people initiated by God. For Arminius, this grace remedied the conflict between original sin and irresistible grace. First, let me establish firmly that God is absolutely the primary or causal pursuer of humankind—Scripture from beginning to end is clear on that. John tells us in First John 4:19 that we love Him only because He first loved us.

First John 4 is one of my favorite chapters in the entirety of the Bible. I call it the "God is Love Chapter" because John masterfully reveals the foundational theology that God *is* love, and not simply a loving God. That the nature of our God *is* love. However, I am not sure that this is a proof text for preceding grace, for one key reason, John is addressing believers and their struggle with fear and love. This is not a statement directed to all humanity. Let's look at it in context:

> *No one has seen God at any time.* **If we love one another, God abides in us,** *and His love has been perfected in us. By this we know that we abide in Him, and He in us, because* **He has given us of His Spirit.** *...Whoever* **confesses that Jesus is the Son of God, God abides in him, and he in God.** *... and* **he who abides in love abides in God, and**

God in him. ...There is no fear in love; but **perfect love casts out fear,** *because fear involves torment* [punishment]. *But* **he who fears has not been made perfect in love.** *We love Him because He first loved us. If someone says, "I love God," and hates his brother, he is a liar; for he who does not love his brother whom he has seen, how can he love God whom he has not seen?* (1 John 4:12-20 NKJV)

John is not speaking into grace, and certainly not preceding grace. The context here is regarding our faith walk and how we are perceiving our own relational position with God. He clearly is writing to those who are already saved and speaking into their lack of love for one another and for people in general, not their salvation. John is pointing out that we love God because He first loved us, most likely referring to his own belief stated in John 3:16, *"For God so loved the world, He sent His only begotten Son...."* Father God certainly initiated salvation because He first loved us.

Personally, I don't believe in preceding grace because I don't believe in total depravity. I lean into the blood of Christ at work on the planet from that day back to the first day and unto the last day. If there is a preceding grace, it was released at Calvary and has not stopped since, nor ever will.

The life is in the blood, so grace that brings life is in the blood of Jesus working in and around us. I also, however, see this grace at work and responded to in the Old Testament, as the blood of the Lamb is a theme and a type, at least from

Moses on, but perhaps even from Abraham and Isaac. The grace to choose Him has always been available to the hearts of those who would respond.

Is Noah lost because he was before the sacrifices of the Law or because he lived a few thousand years too early? I don't think so, his faith has saved him. He believed God. Abraham, Isaac, Jacob, Joseph, Moses, and David all lived before Christ, but they're considered righteous by faith. This simply means that their faith in the Lord gave them right relationship with Him.

Does this mean there is salvation outside of Christ, the Logos, the second Person of the Trinity? No, the One they placed their faith in was the preincarnate Christ. He was the Lamb slain before the foundation of the world (Revelation 13:8). We will spend more time on this topic in Chapter 4.

When I was a young believer, someone gave me a copy of Dr. Arthur Waeterling's teaching on the Trinity. It was absolutely amazing and changed so much of my understanding of the Father, Son, and Holy Spirit. It was my first steps into real theological study, and I loved it. He asks this very profound question: How could a universe with sin present coexist in the presence of a Holy God? I mean, come on, that is a great question.

If "our God is a consuming fire," how can sin survive before His awesome, powerful, perfectly holy presence? Dr. Waeterling gave the answer, "The Lamb slain before the foundation of the world." He shared that the omnipotent, omnipresent, omniscient God put into the foundation of creation the blood of the Lamb slain before anything was created. The atonement was in the fiber of creation, so that sin can, for a season, a relatively short season in the overall scheme of eternity, can coexist with God for God's purposes. This places grace in the very fiber of creation.

God has moved toward humanity in the most profound and amazing ways. He makes Himself known in all He created. He does it in immensely personal and intimate way, and, in fact, He has from the beginning. Scripture testifies to this truth:

> *The wrath of God is being revealed from heaven against all the godlessness and wickedness of people, who suppress the truth by their wickedness, since what may be known about God is plain to them, because God has made it plain to them.* **For since the creation of the world God's invisible qualities—his eternal power and divine nature—have been clearly seen, being understood from what has been made,** *so that people are without excuse* (Romans 1:18-20 NIV).

> *For* **he chose us in him before the creation of the world** *to be holy and blameless in his sight. In love* (Ephesians 1:4).

The language here is very interesting to me. His eternal power and His divinity have been *"clearly seen, being understood"* from nature, so there is *no excuse* not to perceive and choose. To make Himself known and hold people account-able for choosing to reject Him without the grace to rightly choose would be a great injustice. Paul is addressing god-lessness and wickedness in humankind; his teaching here removes the argument, "How could we know?" by saying creation itself reveals the Creator God.

There has always been a grace at work within the frame-work of God personally and intimately reaching out to humanity inviting them to draw close. It has always been by faith and not by works. The evidence of a loving God all around us is sufficient for us to see Him and move toward Him. Whether there is power in common grace to suffice or there is some other kind of additional prevenient grace, is not relevant. What is relevant is that God initiates and provides the means to pursue Him—and those signposts are all around us.

When I was a child, I loved this beautiful Bible my mom had. Our family went to church once a year, at Easter. I had no religious instruction until I was eight years old. But I remember looking at the pictures in that Bible, reading the captions of the great people of the Bible, and feeling drawn to Jesus. Was that His grace drawing my gaze upward to God through those stories? Or simply a child who saw pas-sion in those stories and was drawn to those testimonies and upward to Him? Yes, I believe it was both.

My siblings were also drawn to Him, but in different ways. He has been at work extending us grace from the beginning in all sorts of ways. The invitation is for all. As Paul said to the Athenians in Acts 17, *"in Him we live and move and have our being."* God is and always has been all around us, the evidence of which is undeniable in all we see. He is always inviting people to Him; and through Jesus, He made the perfect invitation complete, unavoidable, and supremely powerful to save all who would say yes.

Endnotes

1. Wayne Jackson, "The True Meaning of Grace" *ChristianCourier. com*; https://www.christiancourier.com/articles/1279-true-meaning -of-grace-the; accessed January 13, 2020.

2. Grace; *The International Standard Bible Encyclopedia*, Vol. 2, 548.

3. Charis; www.biblestudytools.com/lexicons/greek/nas/charis.html; accessed January 13, 2020.

4. Larry D. Sharp, "The Doctrines of Grace in Calvin and Augustine," *Evangelical Quarterly* (April-June 1980); https:// biblicalstudies.org.uk/pdf/eq/1980-2_084.pdf; accessed January 13, 2020.

5. Ibid.

Chapter 2

The Old Testament and Grace

Shaping our world is never for a Christian a matter of going out arrogantly thinking we can just get on with the job, reorganizing the world according to some model that we have in mind. It is a matter of sharing and bearing the pain and puzzlement of the world so that the crucified love of God in Christ may be brought to bear healingly upon the world at exactly that point.

–N.T. Wright

My Grace Journey—Part Two

BEFORE I WAS BORN AGAIN, I valued the Bible, though I had no clue how to understand it. I didn't know what eschatology was, but I know it scared the bejeepers out of me. There were times I would say a little prayer and open the Bible to a random place expecting some mystical encounter that would give me direction. Maybe you can relate. Funny thing is, most of the time, I would come to a Scripture of rebuke toward Israel or some other nation. A stern word of correction or an end-time prophecy. It was like, "Come on, God, give me a break, I just want to know what to do."

I didn't find grace there, I found condemnation. Maybe I was being called to repentance. More likely it is just not the way we walk with Him. As I matured in my relationship and understanding of the Lord, I found those times kind of funny. Thankfully, He loves me and brought me to the place He had for me, right in the center of His heart. Maybe you can relate to my story? We are desperate for answers, something that will make things better. A ray of hope to get us through a difficult time.

What I have found is the only answer, the only answer that works, is Jesus Himself. He is the answer, and His grace is the invitation and the glue that brings it and holds it together. It's His grace that keeps us moving toward life in the fullest, in Him.

In the first days after giving my life to Him, I didn't see grace, the thread of His perfect love, in the Old Testament. I didn't know what to do with that part of God's Word; and to be honest, it scared me. Thankfully, not long after my new walk with Him, that changed. He met me where I was and gave me eyes to see His great love all the way from Adam to Jesus.

I had a pretty radical salvation. If you read my first book, *The Father's Intention,* you know my testimony. When I came to Him, it was the holiday season, once it passed, I got down to business. I had a client in Chicago who was a believer. He was a Baptist, loved the Word, taught the Bible, and was excited to help me get started. He was a cessationist, which means he didn't believe in the gifts of the Spirit for today. I didn't know what that meant at the time, I just wanted to know the Bible.

He suggested I get a New American Standard Bible and the Ryrie Study Bible. I put it on my Christmas list and got it. I was excited and ready to go on this journey with God. I was determined. If God was all Paul Miller said He was, He could teach me, I didn't need a human teacher. I had seen enough phonies in my pursuit of Eastern religions, New Age, and the occult to know I couldn't trust people, at least any I knew. It was going to be me and God or this wasn't real.

My wife Patti was a flight attendant at the time and was working three-day trips. I had plenty of alone time to read, pray, and study. It is funny how I got started the first day on my journey into the Word. I sat in my living room, in my bathrobe, on a cold winter day in early January 1983. With my new Ryrie Study Bible on my lap, I prayed. I'm not sure I could even call it a prayer. I simply said, "Lord, if You are real, and what has happened to me is real, then I don't need a person to teach me. You can teach me. Come Holy Spirit, teach me."

Well, guess what, BAM! He came and started opening up the Word to me with understanding. I started at the beginning. I mean, where else do you start a book? How do you know the plot, the theme, the climax of the story if you don't start at the beginning? So, I started reading Genesis chapter 1, verse 1 and learned that God spoke all into creation. Something ignited in me with the words, *"God said."*

As I read through the Garden narrative and on through the Flood, Abraham, Jacob, Joseph, Moses, and David, I started to feel a shift. Where before all I saw was the God of wrath, now all I saw was the God of love whose lovingkindness endures forever.

I still didn't fully understand the concept of "grace" beyond my experience and the song "Amazing Grace." I understood it was something He did, something He gave to me that allowed me to know Him. But in truth, what I knew was not the theology of grace. I knew the God who is love and His story was jumping off the pages at me. The same God who met me that Sunday morning December 19, 1982, was the One whose story I was reading in the Bible. The God of wrath I was so afraid of slowly vanished in the light of His truth.

Yes, I still saw His judgments on the wicked, but I understood them from the perspective of His love for His children. I began to see that His wrath is against sin, darkness, and evil—not against us. Yes, there is judgment, but His judgment is against sin. He is purifying creation and eradicating sin. Yes, there will be judgment on the wicked, but that is a result of their choice not to repent, not His lack of love. He made a way to come under that purification, through the blood of Jesus. His words jumped off the pages. He was alive to me. He is good. He is love; He is real. I was ruined, ravished, intoxicated by His love; His beautiful, unquenchable, undying love.

Our grace stories, are a collection of individually beautiful pieces of art. Each unique with their own distinct beauty. All filled with the power of our Lord and Savior. When all is done, and all the pieces are fitted together in His story, then we will see just how miraculous it all has been, the artistry of the Master. Our only response then will be to fall on our knees and worship.

Awakened by Grace in the Old Testament

All the expressions of grace were in the Old Testament. The measure was perhaps different. Or perhaps His expression of grace is different. But grace was there from cover to cover from the beginning to the end. God was and still is making Himself known and making a way for all who want a way out of the purification of creation, the judgment against satan and sin. There is no doubt His grace was present, just look at Noah, Samson, Abraham, Moses, and David. The

Lord Most High, is right there in the center of it all. He never left us.

In the Old Testament, He was not an angry God; He was a Father with righteous anger toward sin and those who cause His children to stumble. It was an anger rooted in His passionate, undying, unflinching, immovable love for those who are His. I also discovered that His love was not just for the Hebrew people. His love was for the Gentiles, too. There are two fascinating stories that reveal the grace and kindness of God and His view toward the Gentiles.

In the story of Sodom and Gomorrah, in Genesis 19, we see that Lot had two daughters. The oldest was concerned about their family line dying with them and devised a plan. She and her sister would get their father, Lot, so drunk he wouldn't remember anything. They would sleep with him, get pregnant, and bear sons to continue the family. This sin of incest was indeed a grievous thing, and the offspring were enemies of Israel for hundreds of years thereafter.

The oldest daughter gave birth to a child named Moab; he became the father of the Moabites. The younger daughter gave birth to a son named Ammon; he became the father of the Ammonites. These two tribes were at constant war with Israel. They didn't live in the Promised Land; their territory was on the east side of the Jordan and Dead Sea. They hated Israel and would not allow them to have peace for very long.

There was a woman named Ruth who was married to an Israelite whose mother was Naomi. Naomi had two sons who married Moabite women, Orpah and Ruth. Among the Hebrew people, they would have been looked down on. Over time, both of Naomi's sons died. Naomi heard the famine that caused them to leave many years before was over in Israel and there was now food in Israel, so she decided to go home alone, husbandless and sonless.

Her daughters-in-law started out with her at first, but she strongly discouraged them to journey with her. She told them to go back to their homes and hopefully remarry. This may have been because it would have been almost impossible for them to find a man in Israel who would marry a Moabite woman, especially one who was previously married. They all wept and Orpah returned home. However, Ruth deeply loved Naomi and pledged herself to her. Though Naomi attempted to dissuade her, Ruth makes this amazing statement:

> *But Ruth replied, "Don't urge me to leave you or to turn back from you. Where you go I will go, and where you stay I will stay.* **Your people will be my people and your God my God. Where you die I will die, and there I will be buried. May the Lord deal with me, be it ever so severely, if even death separates you and me "** (Ruth 1:16-17 NIV).

The story goes on to tell how Ruth meets this great guy, Boaz, and how he redeems Naomi's inheritance and with it makes Ruth his wife. So, now there is a descendant of Lot through incestuous relations with his daughter, a Moabite woman, an enemy of Israel, who chooses her mother-in-law's God, marries a good man, Boaz, of the tribe of Judah, and she becomes the great-grandmother of King David. She is remembered in the lineage of Jesus in the Gospel of Matthew. You can find her name in Matthew 1:5-6 (NIV):

*Salmon the father of **Boaz,** whose mother was **Rahab,** Boaz the father of **Obed,** whose mother was **Ruth,** Obed the father of Jessie and Jesse the father of King David.*

Now, look back one verse and you will see Rahab's name. Rahab was a prostitute who helped the spies when Joshua was going to attack Jericho. Rahab married a man named Salmon of the tribe of Judah sometime after the conquest of Jericho. Salmon and Rahab were the parents of Boaz, making Rahab David's great-great-grandmother. These two women demonstrate God's grace and love for Jew and Gentile both.

Consider Bathsheba and David. David has sex, probably forcibly, at least manipulatively, with Bathsheba while she is married to one of his mighty men, Uriah. He then tries to cover up what he's done by tricking Uriah to sleep with his own wife. However, Uriah won't sleep with her or even sleep in a bed while his comrades are at war.

Finally, David sends orders to his commander Joab to place Uriah at the hottest point of the battle and to withdraw support; consequently, Uriah is slain. David then marries

Bathsheba and they have a son who dies in infancy—the judgment David opens the door to by taking Bathsheba and causing Uriah's death. David repents and they are given two sons, Solomon and Nathan. Both of these sons of Bathsheba and David are listed in the genealogy of Jesus—Solomon in Matthew and Nathan in Luke. We can see that the Lord included Jew and Gentile. Jesus came through the line of a prostitute, Rahab, and a Moabite, Ruth. He also was a descendant of an adulterer and murderer, David, and a victim of rape, Bathsheba. What does it say that Jesus came from so many broken people? God's grace, kindness, mercy, and love are obvious throughout the Old Testament. From the very beginning. Where sin abounds, grace so much more abounds.

I started this chapter with stories of grace and kindness from God to drive home the fact that even in the Old Testament, He does not show partiality based on works. These stories and the line to Jesus demonstrate that in God's plan there are no favorites. He routinely uses sinful men and women to complete His redemptive story; and in so doing, reveals the greatness of His love. What do all of these people have in common? Faith!

In Hebrew, the word for *grace* is *chen* also sometimes spelled *hen*. It literally means, "Favor bestowed from a superior to an inferior."

> *Hen* is the "gracious and favorable action passing from a superior to an inferior – an action that

> could not be forced or demanded." Read that
> carefully. *Hen* is pretty close to the Christian idea
> of grace. It can't be earned or demanded. It is a
> sheer gift granted by someone in a superior posi-
> tion by completely magnanimous motives. It is
> poured out on people who have no claim to it.[1]

This is identical to the New Testament *charis,* and demonstrates that grace, the same type of grace, was in the Old
Testament. It is a consistent theme throughout the Bible,
beginning to end. Many believers don't believe grace was
available in the Old Testament. They see the Old Testament as law and the New Testament as grace. That simply is
not true. *Is* there a greater expression and measure of grace
now because of the Cross? Yes, absolutely. But it isn't the
substance of grace, it is the availability and power of it that
comes with the indwelling of Holy Spirit.

The blood of Jesus blew open the doors to grace, but the
favor of God was always available. Now, the living presence
of the God of grace, His Holy Spirit, is alive in us giving us
new life.

Let's take a moment to look at the key issue of grace.
Grace can come in several ways as we already discussed.
However, the grace we primarily think of is saving grace.
Many people think that saving grace was unavailable in the
Old Testament, that simply is not so. When we look at grace
in context of salvation, we need to look at what grace is

addressing or overcoming. What is the victory grace makes available? What does it address?

First, it addresses the statement of law, "The wages of sin is death." That is a law. It isn't said that way in the Ten Commandments, it is a universal and eternal law, like the law of gravity or inertia. They are established and as long as we exist within the confines of this natural realm, they are indisputable laws. We can find ways around them like jet propulsion; but if the fuel runs out, gravity takes over.

When the Lord states, *"the wages of sin is death"* in Romans 6:23, Paul is only articulating what the Lord said in the Garden of Eden. If you eat of the Tree of Knowledge of Good and Evil, the tree that makes you your own god, you will die. Self-centeredness took over and all that God designed us to receive for life from Him was cut off. Because we were created to live by the Spirit of Life, we now must sustain our own lives. God is the only Source of true life, spirit, soul, and body life, but many turn to false gods to get life.

What we worship becomes our source of life. What we worship outside of the Living God is death. Sin brings death, separation from the Lord and each other; it causes and accelerates decay and disorder; it is the beginning of the end. I will talk more about this in the chapter titled "Grace and the Tree of Life." But for now, understand that there is a law that says "sin brings death." However, when sin broke into the world, so did grace and the means to restore relationship with God.

Leviticus 17:11 says that life is in the blood. Scriptures prohibit us to drink blood or to eat any meat with blood in it. Why? Because life is *in* the blood. For us, as Jesus followers, our life is now in His blood, shed on the Cross. So, the shedding of blood in the sacrificial offerings points to His blood and speaks into the means of life to overcome the *"wages of sin is death"* and the Lord from the beginning released a thread of grace to find life in Him. Let's go now to Genesis.

> *Then the man and his wife heard the sound of the Lord God as he was walking in the garden in the cool of the day, and they hid from the Lord God among the trees of the garden. But the Lord* **God called to the man, "Where are you?"** *He answered, "I heard you in the garden, and I was afraid because I was naked; so I hid. ...The Lord* **God made garments of skin for Adam and his wife and clothed them.** *And the Lord God said, "The man has now become like one of us, knowing good and evil. He must not be allowed to reach out his hand and take also from the tree of life and eat and live forever"* (Genesis 3:8-10,21-22 NIV).

What a beautiful story of grace and love. Adam and his wife, Eve, are real people, but also archetypes for all humankind.

> *Therefore, just as sin entered the world through one man, and death through sin, and in this way* **death**

came to all people, because all sinned (Romans 5:12 NIV).

We see here that when Adam sinned, all humankind was brought into a sin state. Now let's go back to Genesis 3. We see that the Lord, Maker of Heaven and earth, comes to the Garden looking for and calling out to the man. The one who had sinned and caused all to be under sin. The Almighty One comes to look for and calls out to him. Do you think the Lord didn't know exactly where he was? Of course not. He isn't searching for Adam; He knows where he is. He is inviting Adam to respond to His call. The Great One, the Beautiful One of Heaven, has just been betrayed and disobeyed—yet His response is to come down and reach out to His children, to call out to them and maintain relationship.

So in the first step of grace, the greater moves toward the lesser. The One who is love moves to the son who rejected His love. They have a clarifying conversation. God doesn't just make it go away. He does not enable sinful behavior; He clarifies it so they can know and understand what they have done. Good parents don't brush away a child's disobedience, they help them understand. Love requires brave communication. Brave communication is not a hard word of discipline without love. No, it is a word of truth with love that allows the person to take responsibility and thereby learn, mature, and grow in wisdom.

After the Lord finds His son and daughter, He unwraps the implications of their decision, what we call "the curse."

I personally don't see it that way, as a curse. They brought this on themselves. I don't see God cursing them as much as I see Him telling them, "These are the ramifications of your choice."

Imagine a son takes the family car without asking, drives too fast, and smashes it. What would a good father say? After he knows his son is okay, he might say something like, "Because you took the car without asking, you don't get to use the car anymore. Because you were reckless, you will work to pay for all the repairs. Your choice shows me I can't trust you; you will need to demonstrate you are trustworthy if you want to restore our relationship to where it was." This isn't a curse; this is the by-product of a bad choice. The father isn't cursing his son, he is teaching him that actions have consequences. However, the wondrous part and the way to reconciliation was already in the fiber of creation, grace through the Cross.

What is called the curse, is God is telling His son and daughter, "By your choice, you have released sin, this is your creation not Mine. I gave you dominion; all of this was under your authority, and you gave that authority to the serpent. With it you have brought death and separation from Me to all your offspring for generations. Because of your choices, this is what life will be like. You will labor, struggle, and toil for what I freely provided you for life. You will feel emotions I didn't want you to feel. You will experience the pain of broken relationships, hopelessness, and division. You will have no access to the Tree of Life to sustain your life, so you will surely die. However, in due season I will bring from the woman a child who will crush the serpent, the devil. He will restore humankind to the place I created for them. I will make a way for you to have fellowship with Me again. Because I still love you, I will rescue you."

Rather than being a curse from God, it is grace from God—as grace was already present.

We also see His love and compassion and grace in Genesis 3:21: *"The Lord **God made garments** of skin **for Adam and his wife** and clothed them."* Blood was shed to cover their sin. A sacrifice was made to cover their nakedness. The Lord shows us two things: sin causes death and the only thing that will cover sin is the sacrifice of innocent blood.

Right here at the beginning of all creation, we are pointed to Christ on the Cross. God makes the first sacrifice for sin with garments of animal skins to cover Adam and Eve's nakedness, to cover the shame of their sinful act. He covers His son and daughter so they aren't naked, ashamed, and exposed. Sin exposes and destroys. Grace covers and restores.

This story might be the most beautiful story of grace in action, the kindness of God to disobedient children, at the very beginning. I say that because it demonstrates right at the start how quick He is to make His way to us. He continues to love us.

In Exodus 34, Moses has already broken the original Ten Commandments tablets. He has been instructed by the

Lord to head back up the mountain to receive new tablets inscribed by the Lord. We pick up the story right after:

*Now the Lord descended in the cloud and stood with him there and proclaimed the name of the Lord. And the Lord passed before him and proclaimed, "The Lord, the Lord God, **merciful and gracious,** longsuffering, and abounding in goodness and truth, keeping mercy for thousands, forgiving iniquity and transgression and sin, by no means clearing the guilty, visiting the iniquity of the fathers upon the children and the children's children to the third and the fourth generation."*

*So Moses made haste and bowed his head toward the earth and worshiped. Then he said, "**If now I have found grace in Your sight,** O Lord, let my Lord, I pray, go among us, even though we are a stiff-necked people; and pardon our iniquity and our sin, and take us as Your inheritance"* (Exodus 34:5-9 NKJV).

There are two key words here: merciful and gracious. First, we have the Lord speaking and declaring He is merciful *and* gracious. The Hebrew word for *gracious* is *chanun* or *hanun*. According to Strong's Lexicon it means to bestow favor, to bend or stoop in kindness to an inferior, to be merciful. The second key word is *gracious*, or *chen*. Again, according to Strong's, *chen* comes from *chanan* and means grace, favor, kindness, etc.

The Lord and Moses are having a conversation. First the Lord states, "I am gracious, I extend grace, favor, kindness; it is in My nature to do so." We can see that Moses fully understands what the Lord is saying because he responds. In modern English, it might read like this, "Lord, if when You look at me, You see me with favor, grace, and kindness, please come with us, though we can be stubborn idiots, please forgive us; make us Yours."

This is an amazing conversation from both sides. The Lord is saying, "This is who I am," and in the context of Israel having just sinned horribly with the golden calf. But Moses, responds, "If this is who You are, forgive us and make us Yours." It is important to note God initiates this conversation. He moves toward Moses—*"The Lord descended in the cloud and stood with him,"* that is the Lord's heart. The response of Moses models how we are to respond, *"pardon our iniquity and our sin, and take us as Your inheritance."* Moses bows but he doesn't go through a list of sins, he simply says, "I believe You, forgive us, and make us Yours." Now look where the Lord takes the discussion.

> *And He said: "Behold, **I make a covenant**. Before all your people **I will do marvels** such as have not been done in all the earth, nor in any nation; and **all the people** among whom you are **shall see the work of the Lord**. For **it is an awesome thing that I will do with you"** (Exodus 34:10 NKJV).*

The Lord makes a covenant with His people—a promise, a bond, an agreement. He is going to do something so amazing with them, the ones who had just rebelled a few days earlier, and the nations watching will be in awe of their God. That is exactly what the Lord desires to do through His children here and now, you and I, to do awesome things that will cause people around us to marvel at His goodness, power, and love.

Abraham and Isaac: A Story of Grace

Due to an illness and malpractice, my wife, Patti, had to have surgery to repair her reproductive system. After the surgery we were told our chance of ever having a child was slim to none. For seven years we wrestled with the struggle of coping with that pain. We had always wanted children. For Patti, it was an assault upon her soul as a woman; not to be capable of having children was a devastating blow. She was fatherless at three years old, and always wanted children and family. This was a dream we both shared. Knowing how much I wanted children made it even more difficult for her.

If you know my wife, you know she has an almost supernatural way with children. They flock to her the way they would run to an ice cream store. However, the Lord had put a promise in me before we received the bad news, before we even knew there might be bad news, in fact before we had given our lives to Him. He put in me the assurance that I would be a father, Patti and I would have a child, somehow it was going to happen.

While doing transcendental meditation, my mantra was Jesus, and I experienced what I realized later was the presence of the Lord. In that moment it seemed as if He was introducing me to my unborn children. I began to weep as I felt this joy; I was going to be a father. Nine months later, we found out we wouldn't have children naturally. I refused to believe it; I knew what I experienced. A few months later we gave our lives to Jesus. One day I was reading the Bible and came across Jeremiah 1:5 (NKJV), *"Before I formed you in the womb I knew you; before you were born I sanctified you."* That was it, it is possible in Christ to have met my unborn child. I knew I was going to be a father to at least one child. Holy Spirit introduced us; I would stand in faith on the promise.

After eight years, we had our son, Jason. We were overjoyed. One morning was I was driving about two hours to work in a hospital in Nyack, New York. I was worshipping as I drove on the Cross Westchester Expressway, when the Lord spoke to me. He said, "Do you love Me?" Of course, my answer was, "Yes, I love You." I was perplexed that He was asking me that question. He then asked me a question no parent wants to hear, "Do you love Me enough to give Me your son?" It was not rhetorical, and it hit me in the deepest part of my soul. He was serious, and I knew there was only one answer.

After weeping for a what seemed like a half hour, I gave the only answer I could, "Yes, Lord. I love You enough to give You my son." I wept a bit more, then peace came over me. That day I went about my business, and over the next few days somehow I barely thought about it. However, I did think about Abraham and Isaac. The Lord required an answer to the same question. I was not Abraham. I didn't feel great faith. I felt broken.

About a week later after visiting friends, we came home and put Jason to bed. As I walked out of his room, I could feel the presence of angels all around us. I looked down from our loft to my wife and niece, Jackie, and asked, "Do you feel that?" Patti said, "Yes, what is that?" I said, "Angels…there are angels all over the room." Jackie said, "I can see them going up and down around us."

We decided to pray. We asked, "Lord, why are all these angels here?" Almost audibly I heard the Lord say, "Preparation." Three days later, Jason became sick, very sick, He had a 106-degree temperature, caused by a little-known disease called Kawasaki. Yes, like the motorcycle. We rushed him to the best children's hospital in the New York area, about 45 minutes away. We had a friend on staff there as a pediatrician. Thus began the worse 72 hours of our lives.

Would our son survive this disease that attacks the cardio-vascular system and can cause aneurysms? Patti now had to wrestle with the same question I wrestled with just over a week before, would she give her son back to Jesus? Whatever happened, would she choose Jesus? She did.

During this time, in my mind the story of Abraham and Isaac rested peacefully in my heart. "The Lord will provide…

my son." That evening, my wife gave Jason to the Lord as two friends, Denise and Joann, prayed with her. I believe the Lord gave us both the grace to walk through that in peace, faith, and love. Jason came through that illness, though he had to walk through some difficult things for ten years afterward. I am blessed to say he is now a healthy 31-year-old with a beautiful son of his own.

And, a few months after we offered back to the Lord our first son, we found out we were to have another son, Matthew. We were doubly blessed. He is gracious and kind.

This easily could have gone another way. Yes, it could have, but the testimony would have been the same. The Lord is faithful to bring us through dark times. He is good. He is faithful. He is loving and kind. Why would He ask this of me? Before I answer that question, let me say this. I have three good friends and a niece who have all lost a child prematurely. I don't believe in anyway I was better or more entitled than them. Nor do I believe the Lord took them. My heart grieves with them deeply.

In all these situations our faith, our friendship, and love for God is challenged. Grace is extended as an invitation and found more fully in our response. It is not a question of whether Jay was restored to us or taken, it was "Is God still good and true?" I will build my life on the foundation of His eternal goodness toward me personally. I wanted to give you a personal perspective on Abraham and Isaac. The pain and anguish, the love and faith, the surrender to His will and His faithfulness to me and mine.

The story of Abraham and Isaac is a redemptive story of grace, a "type" pointing to Jesus, to the Cross. God making away for us to come back. It is a beautiful story of faithfulness and brokenness invaded by grace. Abraham and Sarah, deep in their old age, I mean really old, have a son. A promised son. They were already too old. Abraham stated the impossibility of a man at 90 years old fathering a child. Sarah laughed because she was 80.

I think this next part is kind of funny, and in a way what I have found the Lord does sometimes. Just so the world would know what was about to happen, He makes them wait ten more years. Can you imagine the discussion in the Godhead? "That's so funny, Father. Sarah is laughing now. They think they're too old now, so let's wait ten more years. The joy and the laughter then will be so over the top. No one has ever seen a man at 100 and a woman at 90 have a child." "Yes, Son, it is for the world to experience inexpressible joy. And shouldn't it be so? This is who we are. Joy abounding comes by our grace." I love that story.

Thirteen years later, God calls Abraham to sacrifice his only son, the promised child, to slay him and make him a burnt offering. Abraham didn't know it, but he was about to demonstrate exactly what the God he loved, worshipped, and served would do for the world approximately forty generations later, through Jesus. Let's pick up the story in Genesis 22:

> *So **Abraham took the wood of the burnt offering and laid it on Isaac his son**.... But Isaac spoke*

*to Abraham his father and said, "**My father!**" And he said, "**Here I am, my son**." Then he said, "Look, the fire and the wood, but **where is the lamb** for a burnt offering?" And Abraham said, "My son, **God will provide for Himself the lamb** for a burnt offering." So the two of them went together* (Genesis 22:6-8 NKJV).

Abraham placed the firewood on Isaac's back. Just as Jesus carried the wood that would be His Cross, so Isaac carries the wood by which he will be sacrificed.

I find it fascinating that Isaac calls, *"Father"* and Abraham responds, *"Here I am."* It makes me think of our beautiful Savior on the Cross, crying out for His Father. While Abraham is going to be obedient, I wonder if he thought somehow the Lord would intervene. Whether he did or not, he has come to be obedient and trust God's way to fulfill His promises to Abraham through Isaac.

*Then they came to the place of which God had told him. And **Abraham** built an altar there and placed the wood in order; and he bound Isaac his son and **laid him on the altar, upon the wood**. And Abraham stretched out his hand and took the knife to slay his son. But the Angel of **the Lord called to him** from heaven and said, "Abraham, Abraham!" So he said, "Here I am." And He said, "Do not lay your hand on the lad, or do anything to him; for now **I know that you fear God**, since you have not withheld your son,* *your only son, from Me." Then Abraham lifted his eyes and looked, and there behind him was a ram caught in a thicket by its horns. So,* **Abraham went and took the ram, and offered it up for a burnt offering instead of his son.** *And Abraham called the name of the place,* **The-Lord-Will-Provide;** *as it said to this day,* **"In the Mount of the Lord it shall be provided"** (Genesis 22:9-14 NKJV).

Abraham was being tested as to whether or not he would honor God. The Savior was going to come through this man's lineage. If we don't understand the heart of the Lord and the lesson in this story, this may seem cruel, even abusive. This was a test of worship and obedience. Worship, obedience, and grace are interwoven. Would he choose to love his son—the one promised to him, the one who would father nations, Abraham's promised legacy—more than God?

This is redemption history. These are the natural fore-fathers of Jesus. This story is all about Jesus. But it is also about the choice Abraham makes, the exact opposite choice that was made in the Garden. There are so many things we can worship instead of God. A key to blessing is worshipping God with all of our heart, mind, and strength. This isn't because God is insecure and needs to be built up; no, worship brings life. We will also look at this topic later.

What is the lesson of this story? Of course, it points toward Jesus, but the last line holds the key, *"In the Mount of the Lord it shall be provided."* This is where sustained grace comes to us. What does the mountain of the Lord mean? It is His presence, to be in the place He dwells. For us, He dwells in us, and around us. For us as New Testament believers, the Mountain of the Lord is anywhere we engage His presence. In His presence we find our provision. In this story, the place of grace was found through obedience, honor, and worship. It is solely relational. We carry the Kingdom in us, the Mount of God is in us and we are empowered to make Heaven manifest on earth, to extend His justice, His life, love, and light.

Both Isaiah 2:2 and Micah 4:1-5 speak into the understanding of the Mountain of the Lord. But it is sufficient to say it represents His presence, His government, and His powerful love in action. This all speaks into grace. A grace that has been present and available for all who respond to Him in humility, honor, worship, and love. Grace is certainly to be found in the Old Testament. A book can be written on grace in the Old Testament alone. Here I simply want to establish that grace is woven throughout the tapestry of the Old Testament narrative, from the Fall to Jesus.

Passover and the Ten Commandments: Grace Revealed

If you don't know the whole story of Moses, it is found in the Book of Exodus. He, too, is a type of Christ, and considered the greatest prophet in the Old Testament, a friend of God, pointing to Jesus as the Savior of Israel and all humankind.

Just as Herod tried to kill Jesus as an infant by executing every male child of a certain age in Bethlehem, so Pharaoh executed every infant male Israelite. Moses escapes by being placed in a little reed boat by his sister and is found and brought to Pharaoh's daughter and raised in the palace. Somehow, Moses discovers he is a Hebrew. One day he sees and Egyptian slave master beating a Hebrew and, in rage, kills him. He then flees across the Red Sea to Midian to save his life.

Some forty years later an angel of the Lord, or more likely the Lord Himself in what is called a theophany, appears to Moses and sends him back to Egypt to tell Pharaoh to set God's people free. Moses and his brother, Aaron, go to Pharaoh and there are a series of power encounters with God demonstrating He is clearly the One True God. But Pharaoh will not let the Hebrew people go; they are his slave labor and among the best artisans and workers in Egypt.

The culmination of this power struggle comes when Moses tells Pharaoh, "From your own mouth will come the last plague or judgment." Pharaoh gives orders to kill the firstborn of all the Hebrews, and so with that curses his own people. God makes a way for the Hebrews to be delivered from the spirit of death coming through Passover. Let's pick the story up in Exodus 12.

Now the Lord spoke to Moses and Aaron in the land of Egypt, saying, "This month shall be your beginning of months; it shall be the first month of the year to you. Speak to all the congregation of Israel, saying: 'On the tenth of this month **every man shall take for himself a lamb,** *according to the house of his father, a lamb for a household. ...* **Your lamb shall be without blemish, a male of the first year.** *You may take it from the sheep or from the goats. ...Then the* **whole assembly of the congregation of Israel shall kill it at twilight.** *And they shall* **take some of the blood and put it on the two doorposts and on the lintel of the houses where they eat it. Then they shall eat the flesh on that night; roasted in fire, with unleavened bread and with bitter herbs they shall eat it.** *...You shall* **let none of it remain** *until morning, and* **what remains of it until morning you shall burn with fire.** *And thus you shall eat it: with a belt on your waist, your sandals on your feet, and your staff in your hand. So,* **you shall eat it in haste. It is the Lord's Passover. For I will pass through the land of Egypt on that night and will strike all the firstborn in the land** *of Egypt, both man and beast; and against all the gods of Egypt I will execute judgment: I am the Lord. Now the blood shall be a sign for you on the houses where you are. And when I see the blood, I will pass over you; and the plague*

shall not be on you to destroy you *when I strike the land of Egypt'"* (Exodus 12:1-13 NKJV).

There is so much here for us to consider, but I want to point out a few perhaps obvious points. First, take note they are to sacrifice a young "male" lamb, one without any blemish, a perfect lamb, a perfect sacrifice. They are to make this sacrifice at twilight, as darkness comes upon them. They are to take the blood and place it around the entry where they live. The blood of this perfect, sacrificed lamb over and around the entry to their home, their dwelling, so it will be seen by the angel of death and death will not enter that home. I don't know if any Israelites didn't do this, but I am pretty sure if they didn't, the plague that brought death to Egypt would also have brought death to their household.

Also notice that it was to be burnt, roasted over fire; this was not to be an exquisite culinary experience. No, this lamb was to be eaten with bitter herbs, unleavened bread, and fully roasted. Additionally, they were to eat at the ready, to be able to leave in haste the Egypt of their slavery. To summarize, this points to Jesus, the grace of His great Passover sacrifice for us, and our understanding that we are to take haste in leaving the old country of our slavery behind, and to run as fast as we can from it, not looking back. This story is the most profound "type" in the Old Testament pointing us to Jesus—the Lamb who was slain for the sins of all humankind. But death only passes over those who place His blood over the door to our soul, our heart.

Just as the Passover story is a "type" pointing us to Jesus, the entire wilderness narrative through Joshua and the remaining Israelites taking the Promised Land is a "type" pointing to our journey from slaves to the world, to free sons and daughters of God made to conquer the works of satan.

Making sacrifices to the gods was not uncommon in the ancient Near East; in fact, all the ancient cultures had various sacrifices, including human sacrifices. John H. Walton, in his book *The Lost World of Genesis One*[2] that I highly recommend, shares a very powerful point. All of the ancient Near East sacrifices were made to appeal to the gods, to serve them, even to care for them.

In Hebrew culture, man didn't exist to serve the needs of gods who were distant and saw humans as slaves or less. For the Hebrew, the sacrifices were *not* made to appease a god who saw them as slaves, but rather to restore relationship with their Creator who loved them as His own. The One who loved them had no needs to be met by them; He simply wanted a devoted, loving relationship with them. This is unique in the ancient East, a God who wanted to love and serve His children and was committed to restoring relationship. In fact, I would propose this truth is still rare in the religions of the world today, outside of Judaism and Christianity. The grace of God is at work in creation for this very purpose.

I have already shared the amazing story where Moses receives the Commandments the second time. But let's take a quick and abbreviated look at the Ten Commandments.

I am the Lord your God, who brought you out of the land of Egypt, out of the house of bondage.

You shall have no other gods before Me.

You shall not make for yourself a carved image– any likeness of anything that is in heaven above, or that is in the earth beneath, or that is in the water under the earth; you shall not bow down to them nor serve them. For I, the Lord your God, am a jealous God, visiting the iniquity of the fathers upon the children to the third and fourth generations of those who hate Me, but showing mercy to thousands, to those who love Me and keep My commandments.

You shall not take the name of the Lord your God in vain, for the Lord will not hold him guiltless who takes His name in vain.

Remember the Sabbath day, to keep it holy. Six days you shall labor and do all your work, but the seventh day is the Sabbath of the Lord your God. In it you shall do no work: you, nor your son, nor your daughter, nor your male servant, nor your female servant, nor your cattle, nor your stranger who is within your gates. For in six days the Lord made the heavens and the earth, the sea, and all that is in them, and rested the seventh day. Therefore, the Lord blessed the Sabbath day and hallowed it.

Honor your father and your mother, that your days may be long upon the land which the Lord your God is giving you.

You shall not murder.

You shall not commit adultery.

You shall not steal.

You shall not bear false witness against your neighbor.

You shall not covet your neighbor's house; you shall not covet your neighbor's wife, nor his male servant, nor his female servant, nor his ox, nor his donkey, nor anything that is your neighbor's (Exodus 20:1-17 NKJV).

For the thread of grace we are targeting, I am not going to go into every Commandment and what they mean to us. Suffice it to say, they are all still very much relevant today and hold relational keys for us if we want to walk in friendship and kinship with our Maker.

First, take note that He is the One who delivers us from bondage, in contrast to the one who places us in bondage. This alone makes Him the only One worthy of worship and service. But take it further—in His rescuing us, He doesn't leave us to go the rest of the way on our own. He is intimately engaged in our process, by His grace, to see us through to the finish.

Second, while most do not have carved images they worship, there are still many religions that do. But these are not the only images we can worship. Anything we seek life from is a god to us. It can be money, fame, position, power, drugs, alcohol, sex, and more. Even relationships can be a god to us; we identify them as codependent relationships. Anything outside of Him that we seek to give us life will become what we worship. What we worship we live for and by definition becomes a god to us.

The word *jealous* used in this context does not carry the type of meaning we would generally apply. This is not the jealousy of a jilted lover birthed by insecurity, fear, and rejection. No, this is the jealousy that causes a parent to protect their child at any cost. This is the type of jealousy defined as watchfulness and protectiveness for a beloved child.

I remember hearing an interview years ago with Oprah Winfrey. She said she rejected her Christian faith because, "How could a God who is loving be jealous." She clearly misunderstood the context and was deceived, wrongly applying the instruction of the Word, perhaps from some pain in her life. This is not the jealousy of God. He doesn't need our love, and He loves us whether we love Him or not. It is our response to His love that draws us into His arms, a very safe place to be, a place the enemy will do whatever he can to draw you away from. It is only by grace we can stand, and His grace is powerful.

Do not take His name in vain. What does that mean? In my Catholic upbringing, it meant that we should not use His name in loose conversation. I don't disagree, but I believe it means more. Let's look at the meaning of *vain*.

It is important that we understand the ancient under-standing for names. I unwrap this fairly thoroughly in my book *The Father Intention,* but briefly here. God allowed Adam to name all the animals, and the Scriptures tell us that what he named them defined what they were. Throughout the Bible, we see names are prophetic statements regarding a person. Adam means "mankind," as he is the archetype for all humankind. Samuel means "God heard," speaking into both the fact that God heard his mother Hannah's cry for a child, but also Israel's cry for a king. Isaac means "laughter," he brought joy to his parents in their old age. Jacob means "usurper," speaking into how he would usurp his brother's rightful inheritance. But the Lord changes his name to Israel, "one who wrestles with God and prevails," speaking to the wrestling match he has with the angel of the Lord and the wrestling match Israel would have with God, but God's purposes would prevail. So, there is something significant to name meanings.

In this Commandment, God is telling us not to speak ill of who He is, His character, His heart. He's telling us: Do not speak of Me carelessly or thoughtlessly. Consider your words when you speak of Me. Do not bear false witness to who I Am! If you do, you will bring on yourself the death that comes from being separated from Me.

Finally, He tells us to remember the Sabbath to keep it holy, set apart for Him. While this is somewhat simple, it is also not so simple. When the Lord rested on the seventh day, it wasn't like He was exhausted. No, this speaks to how His purposes were set in motion, the outcome was now certain, everything was in place for His purposes to be realized.

Again, John H. Walton, does a masterful job of unwrapping this in his book mentioned previously. God's desire was to create His dwelling place, His resting place, if you will, His cosmic temple, His home. He did it here on earth and His ultimate dwelling place, His tabernacle, is one of living stones, His sons and daughters in loving union with His Spirit in us. The Sabbath is holy because it is this promise—He will have His rest in us even as we find our rest in Him. This is the ultimate fulfillment of the working of His grace.

> *This is what the Lord says:* **"Heaven is my throne, and the earth is my footstool. Where is the house you will build for me? Where will my resting place be?"** (Isaiah 66:1; Acts 7:49 NIV).

The Lord is saying, indeed commanding, us to make sacred space for us to commune together. Make it the highest priority. He is telling us that He has set this day aside as a testimony of who He is and who we are to Him. We are His beloved and His rest is in us. Our rest is in Him. We are His treasured children, bride, family, and we are at home together. Is this not the most beautiful thing you have ever heard? It is all saturated in grace, and grace is not about merit at all, it is about love and life.

The rest of the Commandments are simply the law of love for all people. If we truly love, we won't covet, steal, bear false witness, murder, or lie. When Jesus says the greatest commandment is to, *"Love the Lord your God with all your heart and with all your soul and with all your strength and with all your mind'; and, 'love your neighbor as yourself'"* (Luke 10:27 NIV), He is summing up the entirety of the Ten Commandments. Grace is love in action; it brings life and peace to us. It is powerful and it is revealed throughout the Old Testament.

Endnotes

1. Skip Moen, "Law and Grace Disguised," *Hebrew Word Study,* December 20, 2011; https://www.skipmoen.com/2011/12/law-and -grace-disguised/; accessed January 13, 2020.

2. John H. Walton, *The Lost World of Genesis One: Ancient Cosmology and the Origins Debate* (Downers Grove, IL: InterVarsity Press, 2009).

Chapter 3

The New Testament: A Greater Grace

But to all who did receive him, who believed in his name, he gave the right to become children of God, who were born, not of blood nor of the will of the flesh nor of the will of man, but of God. –John 1:12-13

Amazing Grace, how sweet the sound that saved a wretch like me. I once was lost, but now am found, twas blind but now I see.

– "Amazing Grace" by John Newton

Jesus: The Provision of a Greater Grace

GRACE HAS SO MANY FACETS, hues, and shades of His love and kindness. It seems that one word is insufficient to adequately or accurately express how the Spirit makes grace known and what it is. I shared previously how I came to Christ. The stunning beauty of the encounter as the words of "Amazing Grace" were sung over Patti and I that morning: "Amazing Grace how sweet the sound that saved a wretch like me." I was acutely aware of my state. I knew I was broken in my sin, but my experience that morning was life, truth, and love.

I wasn't created to be hopeless. I was made for love for Him, and in Him is life. I have lived out of relationship through Jesus with the Father and Holy Spirit ever since. Grace gave me life, not just a physical existence in eternity, so much, much more. My heart came to life with a greater capacity to love, with limitless hope, with expectant joy. Life, His life, was and is still working in me. In fact, the whole world became new as His light became the light of my heart; I began to see the world in a new way.

I have known many believers who have not had that experience or have not been able to hold on to it. Why? I believe over time they stopped drinking of His love and presence. In Ephesians 4:7 Paul writes, *"But grace was given to each one of us according to the measure of Christ's gift."* Paul isn't speaking of the internal working of grace, but rather how God gives to each person according to what is needed to do the job he or she is called to. Paul is unwrapping an understanding of how the government of Heaven is to work in God's family here on earth.

We each have a working in us of the Spirit of God in terms of gifts, talents, wisdom, etc., according to the responsibility entrusted to us. This expression of grace is proportionate to our role in His family. Paul then describes what has become known as the fivefold ministry of apostle, prophet, evangelist, pastor, and teacher. I don't believe that is an exhaustive list; we can see in First Corinthians another list of which only apostles, prophets, and teachers are included from the Ephesians 4 list. Here he adds, *"...then gifts of healing, helping, administrating, and various kinds of tongues"* (1 Corinthians 12:28).

I find it fascinating that pastors and evangelists, but particularly pastors, are not included here. I am not diminishing the role of pastors; their role is integral to a healthy Church family. Those called and gifted for this role are uniquely gifted and graced with a capacity to come alongside the broken with great patience. I am incredibly thankful for them, but without the other gifts, particularly the apostolic and prophetic, we tend to be locked on the needs of people and not on the Kingdom moving forward. We need all the graces of gifts and callings working together. Jesus opened the door for this grace, too. However, this is just one expression of the greater grace provided through Jesus.

In the Old Testament, there are different expressions of grace, as well. The sin offering was a means of forgiving grace. Unfortunately, those sacrifices were only good for a season. Once a year, on the Day of Atonement, the sin offering was made; it covered the sins from the past year. It was insufficient to bring an inside-out transformation, you knew you'd be back a year later to go through it again.

There were also other kinds of offerings and sacrifices each with its purpose, and each pointed to God's kindness to provide for all the peoples' needs. They were designed to remind them who He is and why they should worship Him. They were not sufficient for the kind of reformation that would cause a person to be changed from the inside out. For most it became ritual, not substance. The purpose of all the Old Testament sacrifices and offerings were to point to Jesus.

Jesus came to release to us a far greater grace than we see in the Old Testament. In Him we see a completely new understanding of God's plan for humanity, how He intends to bring His plan to fruition, and a revelation of grace. This new revelation of grace could not be understood and experienced before the Cross. Jesus put an end to *all* sacrifices through His ultimate sacrifice on the Cross. Not just the Old Testament sacrifices, but the need for any kind of sacrifice in order to have relationship with God.

Even today, many Christians still think they must suffer sacrificially in order to have right relationship with Jesus. That is called religious service and it is worthless. This type of thinking tells us that when we offer sacrifices to God, He is more pleased with us. Many see fasting this way and it is made fruitless because of this misunderstanding. Fasting is not a sacrifice to cause Him to come closer. It is a denial of self, so you move closer to Him. He is always right there with you. He isn't the problem with intimacy. The nature of His love is intimacy. The nature of ours is not.

So when we fast, we are commanding our soul to come under the authority of our spirit self, which is in perfect union with God. The purpose of which is to be more aware of His presence in our being and in our life—to know His heart and His mind. Sacrifices made to position us to be made right with God is an insult to the Cross. The work of the Cross is more than enough, that is one of the stunningly beautiful and powerful realities of the *His greater grace* in Jesus.

Jesus: The Revelation of Life

In the beginning was the Word, and the Word was with God, and the Word was God. He was in the beginning with God. All things were made through him, and without him was not anything made that was made. **In Him was life, and the life was the light** *of men. The light shines in the darkness, and the darkness has not overcome it* (John 1:1-5).

I love everything about John the apostle. I love his heart. I love the way he thinks and speaks. I love the simple passion and brilliance of his thoughts and how deeply relational he is in it all. I love, value, and have great respect for Paul, I took his name as my confirmation name when I was 13 years old. Paul is brilliant, I mean genius, and the wannabe philosopher in me loves the way Paul thinks. But I love how John cuts deep into my heart with the love of God. It is John who tells us "God is love."

In First John 4 verses 8 and 16, John tells us, *"God is love."* But in First John 4:16, John reveals something else, we need to abide in Him, *"...God is love, and whoever abides in love abides in God, and God abides in him."* John doesn't say God is simply loving, no. He tells us the very substance and essence of God *is* love and that we are to dwell in Him even as He dwells in us. In other words, even as God lives in us, we need to take hold of the reality that we, too, live in Him.

The idea of being the dwelling place of God is a most important thread in Scripture. I am going to share more on this later in Chapter 7, but I would like to touch on it a bit here. In Ephesians 2:22, Paul says, *"In him you also are being **built together into a dwelling place for God** by the Spirit."* We can see that as a result of the Cross, resurrection, and the choice made when we are born again, we become the dwelling place of God. This is at the core of God's purpose for humankind and it is not often discussed.

When Jesus came and died, we understand He brought the means of redemption. But I am not sure we fully understand what that means. It is hard to simply unwrap this truth, and I am going to do it more fully later, but perhaps a story will be helpful. Hopefully you have had a special house that became a home.

When Patti and I were married just short of one year, we purchased our first home. We went looking for something in our budget, something we could afford. This was not my first purchase, so I had a little bit of an understanding of not judging a house by its appearance. I had carpentry experience and could see potential. We found a 1,600 square foot ranch house with a huge kitchen and lots of little rooms that seemed to be thrown together making the floor plan a bit strange.

However, it was on almost an acre of land, not common in the suburbs of Long Island, less than an hour from Manhattan. And, this was a very big "and" for me, it had a 20x40 built-in pool. YES! It was a few thousand dollars over our budget, but we thought the pros were worth it.

The morning we went to the closing we hadn't been able to inspect the pool or see the house after the sellers moved out. Well, that was not good. We brought it up at the closing and the wife began to go into cardiac arrest. Not really, but it looked like it was a distinct possibility, so we let it go. We closed.

Patti left to fly on a three-day trip, she was a flight attendant at that time, and my mom and I went to clean the house. When we walked in, we were stunned. Without getting into the gory details, suffice it to say, what we thought were minor issues had to be remedied before my bride returned to her first home. Out came the rug, hadn't planned on that, and a new one went in. The bathroom needed to be blown up, black mold everywhere. We made it livable; and when Patti came home, her new home was in semi-order. Mission accomplished. Over the next four years we took it from their home to being somewhat ours. We completed a few renovations that were basically cosmetic. We have some good memories, but it wasn't exactly what we desired.

When Jason was born, we had come into some significant money. We decided this house that we tried to make ours would have to come down and a new one would be built that would become the home where we would become a family. We got together with an architect and designed our dream home. When the demolition company came and tore the place down, I felt no sense of loss. It was a house, it was where we slept, but it wasn't a home. For it to become a home, it needed to be our dream and we needed children living in it.

Several friends and I built our dream house. I put hammer and nail to wood; well, actually nail gun to wood. I put my sweat into it, each day dreaming of the life that would take place there. When we moved into that house some ten months later, it wasn't a house we purchased, it was the home we dreamt of and built. Our one-year-old, Jason, and later Matthew, made it home. It was the life we put into it and the life we lived. It was every Christmas, birthday, July 4th party we had together. It was the touch football games in the backyard that always ended in a tie. It was the laughter, the tears, the love that was there. It was our life in it together that made it special.

When Jesus came, He didn't just come to save us, though I am thankful for His salvation. He came to make a home for His Father by His Spirit. He could have provided salvation without giving us the indwelling of the Spirit of Life. But that was never the plan. It was never about getting us saved. It was always about a people who would be His dwelling place.

This grace that we have is not simply to save us and help us make better choices. It is to make us new, completely different beings from who we were before we received Him. Just like no matter how many renovations we did on our original house, it would never be our true home. It would always be a place where others lived before us. We had to knock it down and build with a new design, new passion, and new vision for it to be exactly where we desired to do life.

Jesus made known God's intention for humankind in that He is the prototype and archetype of the "New Man," and He provided the means to receive His life to us. He didn't simply model the purposes of God for humankind, He didn't come to show us our potential as some religions and philosophies would use His teachings and His life—He came to give us the God who *is* life.

John: The Intimate Purposes of God

In John 1:4 (NIV) we are told, *"In him was life, and that life was the light of all mankind."* The Greek word for *life* here is *zoe*. There are three Greek words for *life* used in the New Testament. First, *bios* speaks of the physical life, our biological life. The second is *psuche* or *psyche*, which is our soul life, the place where our will, emotions, and thoughts originate. Thoughts, emotions, and will have a life of their own. We all experience times when our soul life has caused us to live in ways that were not healthy or good. We might say something like, "My emotions had a mind of their own." What we are saying is they got the best of us and we reacted, we gave life to them. It is where psychology comes from.

Then there is *zoe*. As I mentioned previously regarding the Greek word for *grace*, which is *charis*, all the writers of the New Testament are trying to communicate God's truth with human words. Often, we have to look at the context in order to take hold of the meaning. *Zoe* is the only Greek word used in the New Testament that is always and only translated as *life*. It is, *"The life."* John is stating in John 1 that the Source of true life is God, not just physical, animate life, but the fullness of life.

John makes some interesting statements if we look at both the gospel of John and his letters. First, God *is* love. In John 14:6 (NIV) Jesus says, *"I am **the way and the truth and the life**. No one comes to the Father except through me."* Let's go on a journey together. Jesus is the Word in the flesh. He is the One who spoke as the second Person of the Trinity at the beginning, *"Let there be light."* That Light broke through darkness, chaos, and disorder and established light, purpose, and order. The Light pierced the darkness and brought forth what is necessary for life.

Now remember, God is love, so what we are seeing in the beginning is that God whose essence and substance is love, out of Himself released the key attributes of His nature— love that brings both Light and Life. This is the first act of *grace*. His grace, His love in action, took the darkness and disorder and spoke light and life. You can not separate His love from His Light and His Life. Where there is one there is the other, too.

The word *truth* in Greek is *aletheia*. It means the unconcealed, its application would be "reality." So, when Jesus says, *"I am the truth,"* He is saying, *"I am reality.* When you see Me, not just with natural eyes, but with spiritual eyes, by His Spirit, you see what is truly is the eternal reality. The unshakeable truth, reality." When He says, *"I am life,"* He is saying, *"I am the Source of all true life."* Real life is eternal, what we have without Him is a poor substitute. In Jesus' own words, He is revealing to us several things. First, He is love. Second, He is full of grace and truth. He is the Source of life and is our reality, or revealer of what is eternal everlasting reality.

When God created humankind, Genesis tells us He breathed into man and man became a living spirit, made in God's image. Here we see another expression of grace; God breathed life. Man had done nothing to deserve it, it was even then a free gift. Grace has always been an expression of God's essence and character. Wherever we see His light or truth, His love in action, and or His life moving, we see His grace. John reveals this deeply relational truth of the inseparable power of grace from the Trinity of Love, Life, and Light. These three are the very heart of God, and grace is how they work in us, for us, and through us.

The barrier to grace is fear. Fear kills the workings of grace and causes us to be blind to His love, and the life and light that His love brings to our inner selves. In John's Gospel, chapter 1, John shares some identity clarifiers regarding Jesus. He says first that Jesus is the *Logos,* the Word. He is pointing to Him as the One who spoke at the beginning of time. He then says, *"In Him was life, and the life was the light of men."* John is making known that this is the One who breathed life at the beginning, and now through Him again we can have life.

He is also pointing that this life isn't simply animate life, physical life—this life brings light. This is important to understand. The life He brings exposes hidden things, it causes the hidden things of darkness to be exposed, but it also reveals the hidden things of God. Jesus is the Light revealing the reality of the Trinity and the Kingdom. This life we have in Him shifts our reality from earthy to godly.

Then in John 1 verses 12 and 13, we are told those who believe receive the right to be born of God, not from flesh and blood, but born *of* God, or *from* God. In verse 14, John continues. *"And the Word became flesh and dwelt among us, and we have seen his glory, glory as of the only Son from the Father, full of grace and truth."* The word *truth*, again, is the revelation, the light, of what the eternal reality truly is. Not based on human perspective or understanding, but by the eternal word of truth.

So what does it mean *"full of grace and truth"*? The context can't be properly understood as God's kindness alone. Truth relates to life. I believe the proper understanding of favor or grace is this: God's life by His Spirit working in you. The very breath of God is the great favor, the grace Jesus carries. Grace, God's favor, is seen through love. His love always brings light, reveals His reality, and produces life—His life, godliness and righteousness.

Paul on Grace, Life, and the Future

Paul uses the word *charis* eighty-two times to be exact. In Chapter 1, I explained that there was an application to grace that had to do with power. As a point of reference, I share the explanation again:

> It may be added that in later Greek "charis" also had the sense of force or *power*. It could be a spell, or demonic force, affecting human life with supernatural influences. In Euripides, it was a power from the underworld that could convey the virtues of a dead hero to his living family or followers. This sense, too, though set in a new context, was used in the NT: grace became the

> power of God to enable Christians to live the
> new life in Christ.[1]

It is important to understand the usage of *charis* if we are going to understand the underlying principle of grace. As we look at this word and if we apply it as a *gift,* if we are going to have any applicable understanding, we must ask one question. What is the gift? Practically, what is the gift of grace? The gift can't be the gift. That would be like waking up Christmas morning and there is this beautifully wrapped gift box. Excitedly you unwrap it and in it is something you have never seen before. It looks beautiful, but what's the function?

You say to the giver, "Um, this is pretty and kind of cool-looking, but um, what is it?"

If the response is, "Well, it's your gift."

You may say, "Yeah, I get it, but what is it? What does it do? How does it work? I don't want to seem ungrateful, but what do I do with this?"

It is a gift; but if you don't know what it is or how it works, it's just a big beautiful paperweight. However, if you were told, "This will do any number of jobs for you, all you need to do is press this button and it will do it," now the gift has a purpose and a value. Why? Because you understand not just what it does for you, but why the giver gave it to you. I hope that makes sense. Paul does a lot to help us understand the workings of grace.

In Romans chapter 5, Paul shares on the working of grace in contrast to the death sin brings. Let's look:

> *But the **free gift** is not like the offense. For if by the one man's offense many **died**, much more the grace of God and the **gift** by the **grace** of the one Man, Jesus Christ, abounded to many. And the **gift** is not like that which came through the one who sinned. For the judgment which came from one offense resulted in condemnation, but the free gift which came from many offenses resulted in justification. For if by the one man's offense death reigned through the one, much more those who receive abundance of grace and of the gift of righteousness will reign in life through the One, Jesus Christ.) Therefore, as through one man's offense judgment came to all men, resulting in condemnation, even so through one Man's righteous act the free gift came to all men, resulting in justification of life* (Romans 5:15-18 NKJV).

We are going to look at Romans 5:15-18 again a little later, but I want to spend just a little time looking at it here. Adam sinned, and his sin released death to all humankind. Adam's choice to live without God released death for all. Paul tells us a few things about this first instance of disobedience. First, as Adam's sin released death, so the *free gift* of Christ brings us the means, the power, for life. Not just animate life, but *zoe* life; the divine spark. The eternal life of God.

Paul then tells us, *"those who receive abundance of grace and of the gift of righteousness will reign in life through the One, Jesus*

Christ." The Greek word for *gift* here is *dorea*, not *charis*, and it means a gift given in response to something, perhaps a good act. You might say it is an earned gift. Paul is saying here that the abundance of *charis* AND the gift of righteousness we receive through Jesus causes the rulership of the life of the Spirit in us. He is pointing to a contrast to sin bringing death and *charis* bringing life.

It is safe to say that at least one expression of grace is life, the life of the Spirit that is to be seated on the throne of each human spirit. Sin had ruled in humanity bringing death. But now grace, the gift of God's life, is establishing His rulership within us in partnership with our spirit, for life.

Let's look at one more Scripture passage from Paul:

> *Do not present your members to sin as instruments for unrighteousness, but present yourselves to God as those who have **been brought from death to life**, and your members to God as instruments for righteousness. For sin will have no dominion over you, since you are not under law **but under grace*** (Romans 6:13-15).

Paul, again, is using contrast to provide insight, righteousness and unrighteousness, death, and life. In this Scripture, Paul admonishes readers to get their body, emotions, and thoughts of sinfulness under right authority. Remember, you were brought out of unrighteousness and the death that comes with it into life. In verse 13, Paul tells them that because of Christ they are no longer dead, because with His righteousness we get life.

Then in verse 14, Paul points us to a conclusion that follows the same line of reason and the solution—sin no longer has lordship or power over you, because the law is now powerless, because of grace.

Follow me here, it is an equation. Verse 13 = unrighteousness is to death, as His righteousness is to life. Verse 14 = sin, that brings death, is no longer your master because you are now under grace. Sin leads to death. Grace brings life. We should be able to agree at this point that at least one expression of grace is life—God life.

Love, Life, and the Holy Spirit

At the beginning of this chapter I shared John's thought on God. He says God is love. For God, love isn't an emotion, it is His essence and every functional expression of Him is love. John also tells us God is light. He brings light to darkness, exposing all falsehood. In this we can say the nature of God is perfect truth, therefore He is what is real. Anything contrary to Him is a lie, a falsehood, a deception. Jesus is our reality. It is important that we understand this. The enemy's power over us is rooted in getting us to deny the power, authority, and goodness of God. When we step into that place, we come under the influence and authority of deception.

Also, God is life. Jesus sent to us the Spirit of God, the Spirit of Life. So, in Holy Spirit we have the internal presence of Christ, who said, *"I am the way and the truth and the life"* (John 14:6 NIV). John is pointing to three things: Jesus is love, Jesus reveals the eternal reality, Jesus gives life. All three come and dwell in us by Holy Spirit. Hopefully, we can agree that at least in some cases, grace equals the love, light, and life of God given freely to us and working in us.

You might be saying, "Wow, all of this writing and reading to get here? Really?" Stay with me, there is more, and my hope is it will bring you deeper in love with Him.

Endnote

1. "Grace," *The International Standard Bible Encyclopedia*, Volume 2, 548.

Chapter 4

We Are Not
Totally Depraved

*Fallen man is not simply an imperfect creature who
needs improvement: he is a rebel who must lay down
his arms.*

–C.S. Lewis

AS I SHARED IN CHAPTER 1, the idea of "total depravity" doesn't seem supported by Scripture. If humankind
was "totally" depraved, there would be nothing good found
anywhere. The world would be void of any good outside of
God's working. If that where the case, we would no longer
be image bearers, we would be something else entirely. But
we are still image bearers, though tremendously broken. We
could say that God's grace is working so not to allow for total
depravity to express itself fully, but I don't see it in Scripture.

Even in the first book of the Bible we see in Genesis 4:26, it says in the time of Seth, Adam's third son, *"At that time people began to call upon the name of the Lord."*

Then, of course, there is Seth's descendant Enoch, in Genesis 5:22-24: *"Enoch walked with God after he fathered Methuselah 300 years and had other sons and daughters. Thus all the days of Enoch were 365 years.* **Enoch walked with God, and he was not, for God took him."** Enoch walked with God and then was taken up to be with Him. This doesn't look like total depravity to me. How about you?

Then of course there is Job: *"There was a man in the land of Uz whose name was Job, and* **that man was blameless and upright, one who feared God and turned away from evil"** (Job 1:1). Does that sound like total depravity? In verse 8 of Job, God repeats the same words to satan that Job is blameless, upright, fears God, and turns away from evil. Satan, in his arrogance says, in essence, "Sure, Job's righteous because his life is going great. Let me have him and he will curse You." I believe Job was a real person. I also see this story carrying some significant revelation.

Job was a good man; everything was going well, but he was untested in his faith and maturity. Through his struggles, losses, being falsely accused and judged, he goes through the process that leads him to an encounter with God. In the encounter, he sees the glory of God, he comes to a deeper understanding of the righteousness and goodness of God. That revelation and his restoration in right relationship, positioned him for double-portion blessings. Job became all God desired him to be; he understood God more fully. Again, I don't see total depravity.

We can also look at Romans 1:18-20 that tells us we are able to see and understand the truth of God within the framework of creation. This truth removes all excuses. Therefore, we are responsible for accepting or denying Him. If we were *totally depraved,* as some say, what an injustice it would be to condemn man. It would be like condemning a two-year-old for playing with fire and burning down the house. We are incapable of understanding the ramifications so young. But instead we are told God has placed His fingerprints on and signposts in our natural world in order to lead us to an open door to seek Him.

Saint Irenaeus was the first to write on original sin, in the early second century. He was a student of Polycarp, who in turn was a student of John, the apostle. Irenaeus' understanding of original sin handed down from the apostles to Polycarp, then to him was far different from what most had been taught since the fourth and fifth centuries in the Western Church. Irenaeus didn't see Christ as Plan B, as Augustine and others have. Without spending exhaustive time on this specific topic, let me make just a few relevant points and move on.

- First, Irenaeus saw the Second Person of the Trinity, the preincarnate Christ, as the central point of the creation narrative. The focal point of the Genesis story is not Adam, it is the Son who created all things for Himself.

- Second, the Fall was calculated into the creation as a necessary part of the process for humans to mature and be prepared to be made new in the fullness of Christ's image.

- Third, Adam and Eve were immature and inexperienced. They knew well, because they knew God; but they had no knowledge of evil before the Fall. They were merely naïve, immature children in the Garden. Evil was outside of their experience.

- Finally, there was never a Plan B, everything is as God intended, and moving according to His design.

This is a very brief unwrapping of a very big topic. These points are important for us to move forward.

Augustine and others, long after Irenaeus, saw Jesus as God's Plan B. He was the fixer to man's messing things up. However, the Bible doesn't support that position. Let's look at just two Scripture passages:

- Ephesians 1:4-5: *"even as he chose us in him **before the foundation of the world,** that we should be holy and blameless before him. In love he predestined us for adoption to himself as sons through Jesus Christ, according to the purpose of his will."*

- Revelation 13:8: *"…everyone whose name has not been written **before the foundation of the world** in the book of life of the Lamb who was slain."*

In Ephesians, we are told we were chosen in Christ before the foundation of the world, and in His love, predestined for adoption. Many would argue this supports Calvin's position on predestination, I disagree. Paul, being a Jew, would have seen this as a corporate predestination not individual. He is saying from before the foundation of the world, Christ was already the Redeemer. Theologian Greg Boyd shares this thought:

> In keeping with the Jewish practice of his day, I think Paul was speaking of a corporate election in this passage. When Jews thought of election or predestination, they thought primarily of the nation of Israel. Israel as a nation was elected (not for salvation, but for service). But this didn't mean that every individual born into Israel was part of God's chosen people. Only those who kept covenant with God were considered "true Israelites."[1]

The view that Jesus was the Lamb slain before the foundation of the world is establishing that there is no Plan B. In fact, it reveals that there was no need for a Plan B, as the provision for our restoration was already provided within the framework of creation. The thoughts on original sin as total depravity and individual predestination did not exist in church teachings until the fourth century and later. Even then it was in the Western Church, as the Eastern Church did not adopt this theological position.

Created in God's Image, Even as Sinners

Even today, the Eastern tradition does not have this view. A simple explanation as to why they don't is that we were created in His image. That means our nature carries the potential for good, but we live in a sinful place, and with a corrupted body. It would be like taking a large diamond and sticking it in a pile of manure. The manure changes the appearance and obstructs the beauty of the diamond, it makes it stink; but it does not change the nature, the essence of the diamond.

We are created in His image. We were created good; we still carry the potential of good. Sin clouds the good and it lives in our fallen flesh. However, our spirit still has the capacity for good. If the theology of total depravity was foundational, you would think the apostles would have taught it to the early Church, and so on. If so, we would have a clear record—we don't.

The theology of total depravity and predestination puts many at risk. If we are totally depraved, we can't change our ways. While I agree Holy Spirit is the only One who can completely give us a perfectly new heart, the reality is bad people do, on occasion, change. How is that possible if there is zero percent capacity for good? Predestination leaves many feeling hopeless. What hope do I have for a spouse, a child, a friend—if they are predestined, what does it matter? Why pray if predestined prayer has no effect? Five-point Calvinists would say you pray out of obedience. But when I read the Bible, I see that prayers have an impact. We are told our prayers make a difference. This argument is circular.

A third point, if true, is the Gospel doesn't have the power the Scriptures proclaim. If the Gospel can only move hearts that are preprogrammed for salvation, it really is not all that powerful. The beauty of the Bible is that Jesus died *"once for all."* He shed His blood for every person.

There is a hopelessness and bondage to religion that these doctrines support. A Gospel without hope for all is an empty Gospel, there is no good news in it, unless you are chosen by whimsy to be included. Our God is not whimsical.

Think about this: If we cannot earn salvation, and we can't; it is a gift from God. And if we have no choice, it is luck of the draw, plain and simple. This way of thinking will push us in one of two directions. One, eat, drink, and be merry for tomorrow we may die. Or two, I hope I am in, I hope I am in, I hope I am in. That isn't hope, that is religious bondage to fear. This is not what Jesus taught. It is not what the apostles taught. But it is what a good portion of the Church teaches, and it has been a heavy burden to many.

I have ministered to so many people who have been in religious bondage from this teaching. Please don't misunderstand me. I have met many wonderful brothers and sisters

123

in Christ who are Calvinists. They are earnest, have zeal for the Lord, are faithful servants and deeply loving. I love them and they love me. I personally find it difficult to see how this belief system works in Kingdom theology. When we pray the Lord's prayer that it would be *"on earth as it is in Heaven,"* what does that mean to those unelected? Why pray for the sick to be healed if they are damned to hell? Well, out of obedience; but if they are going to be saved what is the point? No, Christ died for all; all have the potential to choose and be saved by faith. Love requires the freedom to choose. God is love.

Total Depravity Keeps Us Captive

The bondage coming from this teaching took on a new life for me a few years ago. I was speaking at a conference in an area of the country with a long history of Calvinism and Reformed Theology. I was praying for a man to receive a deeper revelation of God's love for him personally. As I was praying, the man got as stiff as a board. I asked him, "What is happening right now?"

He said, "First, I felt like a wall came up and now I am feeling very angry inside."

Interesting, I thought. I prayed and asked the Lord what was happening to cause this. I felt like the Lord said it is a religious spirit coming from the influence of Reformed

Theology in the church he grew up in. I asked the man if that made sense, and he said it did. He said he always thought he was a bad person. His whole life he tried to be good but was never good enough, because he was so sinful. I asked him what he did that made him so sinful. "Nothing, I just am." I asked what the evidence was. He said, "What do you mean?"

"Tell me your sin. Do you curse?"

"No."

"Do you steal?"

"No."

"Do you drink, do drugs, hurt people?"

"No. I try to be good, but I can't."

I asked, "Well what makes you think you're so bad?"

"I must be because I can't experience God. I have never felt His love for me."

That's when I asked him to tell me about his church experiences. He told me he was raised in a church that taught man was totally depraved and only those God chooses get to go to Heaven. We shifted his thinking and prayed again. This time I started with, "I rebuke any religious spirit connected to Reformed Theology."

The man bent over, let out a loud groan, and went limp. I asked him what happened. He said, "I don't know. When you prayed that, it felt like something came right up from my belly and suddenly, I was lighter."

I then prayed, "Father, would You make Your love known to him. Would You give him a revelation of Your sonship and Your great love for him personally?"

Tears started rolling down his face as He experienced the tangible love of the Father for the first time. I saw him the next day and he told me everything seemed to have changed. He slept great, had peace, hope, and joy for the first time in a very long time. I wish I could say I never ran into this type of bondage, but I cannot. It is a fairly common occurrence. I want to be clear; I am not saying those who teach this are bad people. Many, many seminaries teach this. It has a strong tradition and traditions are hard to let go.

Saints, Not Sinners

Another perspective that often goes with this teaching is that we are still sinners saved by grace. I would say to that yes, I *was* a sinner saved by grace. I am now a *saint of God* who struggles with sin. When you place an *I am* in front of a statement, you are making an identity statement. *I am* is a defining term to speak into the nature of a person. I am a father. I have an identity as a father. Jesus died for me. He died to set me free from the bondage of sin. That bondage is established in my self-view, how I see myself. How I see my self-worth is tied to how I see myself. If I see myself as rejected, I will see myself as small and unlovable. If I am affirming to myself that my identity is sinner, I will expect less of myself when I sin. When I fall, I will say, "I can't help myself; I am just a sinner."

Our identity affects all our choices, our response to failure and conflict, the value we put on ourselves to be better people, are all impacted by our identity. The Bible communicates a very different perspective. I truly do not understand how we still see this view in the Church. Not once in all the letters of the apostles are we referred to as anything other than saints. Not once are God's people called sinners in the present tense. *We were once slaves to sin. While we were yet enslaved to sin.* These are the statements we see but none are present tense.

> *For through him we both have access in one Spirit to the Father. So, then* **you are no longer strangers and aliens,** *but* **you are fellow citizens with the saints and members of the household of God** (Ephesians 2:18-19).

Answer this question: If we are sinners, how can we be included in the household of God? If we are hidden in Christ, how can we still be sinners? We are saints, set apart for God as a royal priesthood of sons and daughters of the Living God. This grace of God isn't just a kindness, it is His very presence and power. We are free from the religious lies of the depraved sinner identity. In fact, we are so far removed from it, we should be less tolerant of unloving choices and more understanding of the power of grace for all the saints, and for the lost as well.

Endnote

1. Greg Boyd, "How do you respond to Ephesians 1:4-5?" December 6, 2018; *ReKnew.org;* https://reknew.org/2018/12/how-do-you-respond-to-ephesians-14-5/; accessed January 15, 2020.

Chapter 5

The Tree of Life and Grace

The Son of God became a man to enable men to become sons of God.

–C.S. Lewis

I REMEMBER MY MOM'S BIBLE when I was a child—a beautiful 12x18 gold inlaid Bible with beautiful pictures of Bible stories. One was Adam and Eve in the Garden of Eden. There was the Tree of Life with beautiful golden leaves. And not far off was the "other tree" with a serpent in it. I remember thinking how beautiful the Tree of Life was and how the other tree was not. In a child's mind, I thought, *Eat from the pretty tree, eat from the pretty one and you won't die.*

I had a fear of death from a young age. Maybe because my great-grandmother died a few weeks before I was born and how hard that hit my mom, who was her favorite, while I was in the womb. Or maybe it is because I almost died at birth, but I remember thinking, *Eat from the pretty tree and have life.* There are some important points to be made from the story in the Garden beyond Adam and Eve eating the apple. Let's look at a few Scriptures together and then unwrap those points a bit.

> *And the Lord God planted a garden in Eden, in the east, and there he put the man whom he had formed. And out of the ground the Lord God made to spring up every tree that is pleasant to the sight and good for food. The* **tree of life** *was in the midst of the garden, and the tree of the knowledge of good and evil* (Genesis 2:8-9).

> *...Now, lest he reach out his hand and take also of the tree of life and eat, and live forever* (Genesis 3:22).

A few points of reference: God made a garden, a place specifically created for humankind. It was a beautiful place full of all good things. It was made from love and God would walk with man in this place. In the garden He placed all types of beautiful trees with fruit for eating. Nutrition to provide sustenance for the physical body. But He also placed two other trees in the garden. One is associated with life and the other death. There was perhaps apple, peach, plums, pears, and more. We know there were fig trees, as Adam and Eve covered themselves with large fig leaves (Genesis 3:7). There were probably some trees there we can't even imagine the beauty or flavor of their fruit. These two trees were unlike any of the other trees not specifically mentioned. These trees had a fruit that was not for the sustenance of the physical body.

Grace and Life—Connected From the Beginning

I have found so many Christians who believe Adam was created to live forever. The thought is, "If he didn't rebel, he would have lived forever." Seems reasonable, except it isn't true. Would he have had an incredibly long life? Probably, maybe even a few thousand years. Who knows? But eventually he would have died. If he was created to physically live forever, why would there be a tree of life? The answer to this question is important to understanding God's amazing plan for humankind.

We can see the fruit of these two trees were different from all the other trees. How are they different? Why are they different? We know that the Tree of the Knowledge of Good and Evil brings death. But they didn't die. They lived for hundreds of years. What makes you think they weren't already moving toward death. If they were created to live forever, why the Tree of Life?

The question is, what kind of death is Genesis pointing to? Is it bodily death, spiritual death, some other kind of death? The answer to this question will bring light to many other things regarding God's eternal plan for humankind. We can see even after Adam and Eve sinned, they could eat the Tree of Life and potentially live forever in their fallen state. God in His mercy doesn't allow that to happen. In His mercy He removes them from the temptation. But what is this death then? Is it a lie? Did the Creator lie to them? The key to understanding the meaning of, *"for in the day that you eat of it you shall surely die,"* is in the Hebrew language.

> *And the Lord God commanded the man, saying, "You may surely eat of every tree of the garden, but of the tree of the knowledge of good and evil you shall not eat,* **for in the day that you eat of it you shall surely die"** (Genesis 2:16-17).

It is common in Hebrew writing to repeat the same word twice. It can mean pay attention, an emphasis on the seriousness of what is said. It can also mean the guarantee of the process that will bring you to the inevitable conclusion. The Young's Literal translation gives us some insight: *"... for in the day of thine eating of it–***dying thou dost die.***"* This means that on the day you eat this fruit, the inevitability of the outcome is set. You will die. There is no turning back. Your spirit will experience death immediately as will the great intimacy of our relationship.

We see the reality of these words in the aftermath—for the first time they experience shame. Shame is self-hate; the incapacity to love yourself rightly. Healthy, humble love of self is necessary to walk in fullness. We *must* love what God loves, that begins with healthy self-love. Healthy self-love is void of pride. It is humbly honoring God and people. It is not insecure. At the moment of their rebellion they experienced for the first time death to their innocence and intimacy. They had a paradigm shift and at the core of that shift was their self-view—shame. The second part is physical death is accelerated toward its finality. There is no turning back from the cause and effect of their choice. Physical death is now an inevitable conclusion.

The Tree of Life was the means of grace in the Garden. This grace must be in the very fiber of creation. If Christ is the Lamb slain before the foundation of the world, if we were predestined *in* Christ to receive the Spirit of adoption, the plan of God was always for the second Person of the Trinity to be the means of grace. Christ has always been the vehicle of grace and the Holy Spirit has always been the substance of grace. Not just saving grace but sustaining grace.

The Tree of Life and the Bread of Life

Clearly the Tree of Life was a source of eternal life; we can clearly see this truth. When we look at the full landscape of Scripture, we can see the provision of grace was present from the beginning. I find it fascinating that the Tree of Life appears physically in only two places. First in the Garden and then in the New Jerusalem. There is amazing revelation that comes from looking at this tree. In between Genesis and Revelation, the tree is only mentioned in Proverbs. In Proverbs, we gain an understanding of what the fruits of the tree are. Let's look at those verses. First, in Proverbs 3, the wisdom chapter, we see the fruit of wisdom. God's life produces the fruit on the Tree of Life.

> *She* [godly wisdom] *is more precious than jewels, and nothing you desire can compare with her.* **Long life is in her right hand; in her left hand are riches and honor.** *Her ways are ways of* **pleasantness,** *and all her paths are* **peace.** *She is a tree of life to those who lay hold of her; those who hold her fast are called* **blessed** (Proverbs 3:15-18).

Here we have a list of what the tree produces for us. First mentioned is *long life,* there is a connection between living in godly wisdom and life span. Here are a few verses that support this truth:

- Deuteronomy 5:33 – *You shall walk in all the way that the Lord your God has commanded you, that* **you may live,** *and that it may go well with you, and that* **you may live long** *in the land that you shall possess.*

- Proverbs 16:31 – *Gray hair is a crown of glory; it is* **gained in a righteous life.**

- 1 Peter 3:10 – *For* **whoever desires to love life and see good days,** *let him* **keep** *his tongue* **from evil** *and his lips* **from** *speaking* **deceit.**

- Proverbs 10:27 – **The fear of the Lord prolongs life,** *but the years of the wicked will be short.*

- Ephesians 6:2-3 – *"Honor your father and mother" (this is the first commandment with a promise), "that it may go well with you and* **that you may live long in the land."**

- 1 Kings 3:14 – *And if you will walk in my ways, keeping my statutes and my commandments, as your father David walked,* **then I will lengthen your days.**

We can see in these verses there is a correlation between obedience to living God's way and life span. I understand that we still live in a sinful, fallen world and there are times people who live a life of love, pursue righteousness, and honor of God sometimes still die young. I can only say we live in this place. But I also see men like Billy Graham, Smith Wigglesworth, Charles Finney, and others who lived long lives, especially according the medical abilities of their time.

Yes, there are others who have died prematurely; I cannot be the judge as to why. Spiritual warfare is a reality and, of course, the practical choices of good health. However, the key point is if there is scriptural support, if we live within the guidelines of God's Word and way, we have the promise of a long, full life. I want to preach, teach, and demonstrate the Kingdom with signs and wonders into my late eighties or early nineties; and when I can't do that any longer, go home.

In Revelation 2:1-7, there is a fascinating point made by the Lord. He is addressing the Ephesian church. He first lists all the things they are doing well. They worked hard for the Gospel; they hated evil. They tested every so-called apostle weighing through to see if they were true. (Obviously this is not regarding the Twelve, there were others recognized with apostolic callings and gifts.) They were diligent to weed out the false ones. They patiently endured persecution without giving in to the pressure to stop making the name of Jesus known. These are all really good attributes of a community.

But there was one thing that they were lacking, and this one thing was enough to cut them off from the freedom to eat the fruit on the Tree of Life. What was this one thing? *"But I have this against you, that you have abandoned the love you had at first"* (Revelation 2:4). Their religion was proper, but they were not pursuing the intimacy of first love. Verse 7 reads, *"...To the one who conquers I will grant to eat of the tree of life, which is in the paradise of God."* There is a connection between the love connection with Jesus and the capacity or ability to receive His life in us. This can't be underestimated. Without intimacy, there is a lack of the expressions of His life in us and through us.

When I came to the Lord, I would meditate on Him and His Word for extended times daily. In fact, most of my personal theology came from my study of Scripture during these daily times of meditation. Surrendering my heart in intimacy released life in me. I found the transformative power of that consistent act of surrender, intimacy, and rest in Him empowered me with peace and wisdom. That posture radically changed my life.

When I am too busy with ministry and life, allowing for those regular first-love times with Him to slide, I feel the slow death in my heart. I become impatient, curt, cynical, and will lean into isolation. Intimacy, the act of surrender to the One who *is* love, leads to greater life in our soul. You can't separate His love from His life flow.

There is another fascinating statement made in Revelation 22 that is worth looking at to gain some understanding of what the fruit of the Tree of Life is.

> *Then the angel showed me the river of the water of life, bright as crystal, flowing from the throne of God and of the Lamb through the middle of the street of the city; also, on either side of the river, the tree of life with its* **twelve kinds of fruit, yielding its fruit each month. The leaves of the tree were for the healing of the nations** (Revelation 22:1-2).

Note that the Tree of Life is now back in the picture. It is a tangible, material reality and it produces fruit. Of course, if you take Revelation as prophetic allegory, this isn't literal. Whether it will be a physical reality or this is allegorical and speaking into how the fulfillment of age will work in a spiritual dynamic isn't relevant for this conversation. So, let's not get caught up in that.

Notice there are twelve fruits and it will never stop bearing fruit in every one of the twelve months. But the fruit is not the only noteworthy part of this tree, its leaves also have great value as they bring healing and restoration to the nations. The Tree of Life straddles both sides of the River of Life flowing from the throne of the eternal Christ. The river flows out from the New Jerusalem to the world.

Note that there are twelve fruits to the tree. The number twelve is the number of God's government. The fruits are the fruit His Life, His essence, which not only will govern over every person, but His government will also reside in His sons and daughters. We will carry and radiate His love, light, and life. I know perhaps that can seem confusing. I am going to discuss this more thoroughly over the next two chapters, but for now let me give just a little clarity.

His Government Is Built on His Love

The government of God is not one with layers of laws, stipulations, rules, and regulations, as we may think of government. His Kingdom is not a bureaucracy. His government is established upon His unshakeable and unchanging love. When His love is dominant in us, we become the Law of Love fleshed out to the world. We become the Light of the Kingdom to the world. We become the Givers of Life we were created to be.

The Ten Commandments were not intended to be a law of good behavior, they define for us the law of true, godly love, and in doing so, reveal our need for God to transform us from the inside out. The Commandments start with loving God; coming to Him in worship is how we engage in intimacy and how we appropriate His life. They move from being God focusing us upward, to teaching us what love looks like, focusing us outward toward relationships with people. God is deeply relational. If you love God thoroughly, you will honor your parents. You will hold them in high esteem. You will serve them with love, patience, and kindness, etc. If you do, you will have long life.

Then the Commandments define what love looks like in all other relationships. If you love whom God loves, you won't steal, covet their possessions, lie about them, and so on. It is the Law of His love. His love is what the government is founded on. In fact, His love *is* the government of Heaven. So, the fruit of the Tree of Life is the fruit of His love and the leaves, the life of this tree will heal the ethnicities of the world. The word "nations" in Greek is *ethnos,* or races. The leaves heal the division that sin has caused. The fear and animosity between the races. His life in His people unites us as one people—His family. All people together as one in Christ. This all speaks of His government and the power of His love, light, and life working in eternity for and through sons and daughters.

The Intimacy of God and the Intricacy of His Purposes

When we look at Genesis 1 through Western, scientific eyes, we tend to look at the logic of how God made things as opposed to the purpose. Our Father is very purposeful in all He does. His plan is not simply scientific. He can make the science work in any way He chooses to fulfill His plans. If we remove the Western mindset and how we analyze Genesis 1 into a more Eastern, particularly ancient Eastern, way of thinking, we can start to ask some deeper and more important questions. When we fix our study on the how and proving the how, we can miss the why.

I would present to you that the why is more important than the how. At least in a practical way. How God created the material world is not nearly as valuable as how He created things to work in relationship to Him and His children. The more fruitful questions for us may be the following: When He created His creation, particularly humankind, how did He design it to interact with the Creator? Are there principles He built into the systems of creation that are integral to everything working according to plan? There must be, right?

If a designer were to design a new more efficient engine, he would have to consider the most efficient fuel and system to maximize the energy output of the engine. That would be dependent upon the purpose of the vehicle the engine will serve. Is it a car, a plane, a train, a boat, or perhaps some new type of vehicle? The point is the purpose would determine several factors in the building process. If we know the purpose, we can more easily understand how it works. So, the why will impact the how. Makes sense.

We have been so caught up in defending the creation narrative occurring in a literal 24 hours that we often don't discuss *why* God made everything. If we understand the why, we will be able to focus on the *how* and that will lead us to truth. From my humble perspective, whether the Lord created everything in a literal 24 hours is secondary to why He did it. What is the plan? Where is He taking it? What is He building? I want those answers because the answers to those questions help me understand Him and my place in the created universe.

Let's look at the how God made things work in an orderly functional fashion. How creation intended to work. First, He desires interaction with His creation. Our God is not a God of distance, He is not a faraway God. He made things for Him to be right in the middle of it all. Bumping elbows with His creation, particularly His kids. Getting down into the soil with us, partnering in creating things. Creativity is part of His nature He clearly put in us. So, He wants to be in partnership with us.

From the time my oldest son, Jason, was about 5 to 11 years old, he loved to go to work with me. It didn't matter what type of work I did, he wanted to come along. I was bi-vocational for more than twenty years. During that time, I worked countless jobs. I delivered newspapers; Jay helped a few times. I repaired and restored leather furniture; again Jay came and helped from time to time. I loved having him with me, not because he made my work easier, certainly that wasn't the case when he was very young, but because I wanted intimate, relational time with him. We share some fond memories of the rides in the car, the people we met, the games we played during the day. We were doing life together.

That is one of the many purposes of God. He is love; love is relational, it is intimate, it is life-giving. Of course, we don't give Him life, but we do give Him joy, and joy is an expression of what He intends for life to be—joyful.

> *For I know the plans I have for you, declares the Lord, plans for welfare and not for evil, to give you a future and a hope* (Jeremiah 29:11).

Jeremiah 22:11 tells us that the Lord has great plans for us. While the context of this was an encouragement that they would be set free from captivity, it also speaks into eternity's future for us. Forever, all the intentions of the Lord are filled with hope, beauty, joy, and love.

It is also God's intention to make Himself known through us, not just to the world, but to angels. Paul wrote:

> *To me, though I am the very least of all the saints, this grace was given, to preach to the Gentiles the unsearchable riches of Christ, and to **bring to light for everyone what is the plan of the mystery hidden for ages in God**, who created all things, so that **through the church the manifold wisdom of God might now be made known to the rulers and authorities in the heavenly places.** This was according to the eternal purpose that he has*

realized in Christ Jesus our Lord, in whom we have boldness and access with confidence through our faith in him (Ephesians 3:8-12).

We can see here that part of God's plan was that in this age, the Church, His sons and daughters, would reveal something of His great wisdom being made known to authorities and rulers in heavenly places. Part of His intention is, through His children, those dwelling in heavenly places will learn something about Him they had not yet understood. Another purpose in His plan. How is that going to happen?

For this reason *I bow my knees before the Father,* **from whom every family in heaven and on earth is named,** *that according to the riches of his glory he may grant you to be strengthened with power through his Spirit in your inner being,* **so that Christ may dwell in your hearts through faith,** *that you,* **being rooted and grounded in love,** *may have strength to comprehend with all the saints what is the breadth and length and height and depth, and to know the love of Christ that surpasses knowledge, that* **you may be filled with all the fullness of God** (Ephesians 3:14-19).

The reason Paul prays is so His family, God's family, the Church, will be filled with Christ through faith, for His love to be so deep in us, the very foundation of our lives, so we will live knowing the fullness of His love to the point of being completely filled to *"all the fullness of God."*

Another purpose of God is to have a family that is just like Him. I don't know what it is to be filled with all the fullness of God, but I am hopeful and confident I will experience it this side of Heaven. This is another purpose of God for humankind.

For now, these purposes are enough to grasp hold of the truth that intimacy with God is part of the intricacy of His purpose. Within the complexity of His plan lies the foundation of intimacy, the closeness, confidence, and familiarity of His love. The same exact essence and substance of the love that *is* the Godhead. We are being brought into the familial relationship that exists between the Father, Son, and Holy Spirit. But only as we partake of them do their love and life become the light we live by. This is the grace of God; He gives us Himself and He is enough.

Chapter 6

Living by Grace— Christ in Us

But the free gift is not like the trespass. For if many died through one man's trespass, much more have the grace of God and the free gift by the grace of that one man Jesus Christ abounded for many. And the free gift is not like the result of that one man's sin. For the judgment following one trespass brought condemnation, but the free gift following many trespasses brought justification. For if, because of one man's trespass, death reigned through that one man, much more will those who receive the abundance of grace and the free gift of righteousness reign in life through the one man Jesus Christ (Romans 5:15-17).

I HAVE CALLED THIS CHAPTER "Living by Grace— Christ in Us." I bet when you read that title you didn't question whether the Bible says we live *by* grace. It is not unreasonable to think that it does. But the Bible doesn't tell us to live by grace. It does say in Second Corinthians 5:7 we are to walk by faith and not by sight. Simply meaning God's word, His promises, trump our emotions or what our natural eyes may tell us. However, it doesn't say to live by grace, though it sounds good. So why did I title this chapter that way? That is what I am hoping to unwrap for you. Remember, my thesis or key point of this book is that at least in certain verses, we see grace as the life of the Spirit working in us.

In Chapter 3, I used the same verses from Romans as here. I explained there was another Greek word for *gift* other than *charis*. You might remember I shared the word *dorea* meaning a gift given in response to something. It is sometimes translated as a gratuity. You might miss something if you don't look at the meaning of the Greek words. In verse 15, we see in English "free gift"; the first time we see that phrase the word in Greek is *charis* not *dorea*. *It is* speaking of the freely given gift, grace, that brings life.

The word *dorea* appears in the second part of this verse. It says the *dorea*, response gift, by the *charis* of one man. However, in verse 16, the first time you see "free gift," it is translated from *dorea*. The second time you see *free gift* it is translated from *charis*. This can be very confusing, so why does it matter? Let me write it in a way that may be easier to understand:

But *the free gift is not like the trespass.* For if many died through one man's trespass, much more have the grace of God, and *the free gift* by the grace of that one man Jesus Christ abounded for many.

This freely given gift, no strings attached, is not in response to your sins. While sin was a response to a choice. This gift is not a response caused by our actions. If sin was a response to a choice that brought so much death, how many more will receive life from the responding action, the gift Jesus gave through His favor; the free gift of His life, His love.

> *And the free gift is not like the result of that one man's sin. For the judgment following one trespass brought condemnation, but the* **free gift** *following many trespasses brought justification* (Romans 5:16).

The gift is the free gift of Christ, this is far greater than the condemnation and death sin released. This gift that is Jesus overcame *all* sin, bringing justice to sin itself, releasing the free gift of life for those who receive Christ rightfully.

> *For if, because of one man's trespass, death reigned through that one man, much more will those who receive the* **abundance of grace** *and the free* **gift of righteousness reign in life** *through the one man Jesus Christ* (Romans 5:17).

If one man's sinful choice released death as master over all, how many more will have life because of the limitless extravagance of the gift of life Jesus gives. Once received, His free and extravagant gift of life doesn't stop there, when we respond with our yes, we receive the gift of restored friendship with God; all things are made new in Christ. Now, as royal sons and daughters, completely forgiven, walking in peace with our Father in perfect fellowship, we get the life we lost back, the life He intended for us at the very beginning.

Whom the Son sets free is free indeed. If we are set free from sin and death, what is the trade-off? For sin, we have received perfect love. For death, we have received the fullness of life, both are in Jesus Christ. Both are packaged in the gift of grace.

The Life of Christ in Us

In John 14, Jesus shares that He will ask the Father to send the Helper. We know the Helper is the Spirit of God. Jesus begins with a statement:

> *If you love me, you will keep my commandments. And I will ask the Father, and he will give you another Helper, to be with you forever, even the Spirit of truth, whom the world cannot receive, because it neither sees him nor knows him. You know him, for he dwells with you and will be in you* (John 14:15-17).

In the first line we have the Gospel message. Love Jesus, and if you do, you will keep His commands. What are those commands? Very simple, love God and love people, without question, freely even as He loves us freely, despite all our junk. If we will do that, commit to Him, we will get the Helper, the Spirit of Truth, and the Spirit won't simply be *with* us, but will *live inside* us.

> *To them God chose to make known* **how great** *among* the Gentiles **are the riches of the glory of this mystery, which is Christ in you, the hope of glory** (Colossians 1:27).

I love this verse, it is both amazing and beautiful. How is Christ in us? By the Holy Spirit, of course.

There are many names for the Holy Spirit, I want to list just a few here:

- Spirit of God
- Spirit of Truth
- Spirit of Adoption
- Spirit of Power
- Spirit of Life
- Spirit of Love
- Spirit of Wisdom

We should know that Holy Spirit is God. Whenever we see Holy Spirit moving or doing something, we are seeing

God. He is also the Spirit of Truth. We discussed earlier that this word "truth" can best be understood as making the unseen seen, reality. Holy Spirit makes the hidden things of God known to those who love Him.

He is the Spirit of Adoption; whenever a person receives Christ as Savior, the Holy Spirit comes to bring the Father's love. He brings us into the family. He is the Spirit of Power. Holy Spirit moves powerfully in countless ways. In salvation He changes the sinner's heart; in healing and deliverance, He breaks the power of darkness with the superiority of His life, light, and love. He *is* the Spirit of Life, because He is life itself. There is no life, true spiritual life and health, without the Holy Spirit. He is love, obviously because the very nature of God is love; Holy Spirit is the Spirit of God. And He is the Spirit of Wisdom, because in Him is *all* understanding of all things as all things were created through the power of Holy Spirit.

What I want people to understand is that all these Holy Spirit identities are in every believer, because the Spirit lives in us. Christ is in us by the very indwelling of the Spirit of God. We have access to all this and more.

The Power and Joy of Communion

We can't overestimate the value and power of communion. The Oxford Dictionary defines *communion* as "the sharing or exchanging of *intimate* thoughts and feelings, especially on a mental or spiritual level." Communion is very intimate. In the Godhead, there is perfect communion. There is also a *covenant* relationship. A covenant is a legally binding agreement. It is a contract of law with stipulations two or more parties agree to. It will have guidelines and stipulations, with consequences spelled out for breaking the covenant.

Communion and covenant come together in marriage. It is fascinating to see how many times the Lord refers to Israel in the Old Testament through the lens of the *marriage covenant*. When the Spirit of God led the Hebrew people from Egypt, once they were safe, He gave the Law. The Law was a list of dos and don'ts, with spelled-out consequences if it was broken. If you take a good look at the Law, it was a marriage contract, or perhaps a prenuptial. The focus is maintaining right, good, loving relationship with God. The key relationships were identified as His people, His children, His bride, and a few others, but these suffice for now.

The purpose of the Law was to spell out what would maintain fellowship with God and what would break it. You don't need to get too far into the Old Testament to see Israel had a very hard time staying faithful to this covenantal agreement. As a result, communion was broken countless times. Each time they would suffer the consequences, the very ones spelled out in the Law. Each time after a season, God, who was a jilted lover, would pursue them and remind them of what they did to bring them to their current circumstances. They would repent and communion was reestablished, the covenant restored. Communion and covenant go hand in hand.

The most common theme in the Old Testament for the covenantal communion relationship with God is marriage. He often declared and rebuked Israel for acting adulterously with foreign gods and nations. In fact, He had the prophet Hosea marry an adulterous woman as a living, breathing representation of the relationship of God with Israel. Marriage is one of the most integral relationships God ordained to make Himself known. Another is that of father and child. He is very family oriented.

In marriage, there is only one thing that can violate covenant and legally release one party from the other—sexual immorality with a lover outside of the marriage. Adultery is the only legal violation that releases the parties. Why? Because of the communion factor. Communion is the bond of transparent, vulnerable, binding love that allows for trust, safety, covering, and rest in the relationship. When trust is broken with an unloving act of giving oneself to another lover, the relationship is no longer safe, vulnerable, restful, or life-giving. It can be restored, but only when the party who violated the covenant, repents, takes responsibility, and works to restore trust.

In Romans 7:1-6, Paul is teaching on the bondage of the Law in comparison to grace-given life:

> *A married woman is bound by law to her husband while he lives, but* **if her husband dies, she is released**

from the law of marriage. Accordingly, she will be called an adulteress if she lives with another man while her husband is alive. But if her husband dies, she is free from that law, and if she marries another man, she is not an adulteress (Romans 7:2-3).

Paul is explaining that if your relational connection with God is the Law, or religious observances, you are bound to live by the Law, though powerless you are to do so. He is pointing at the husband in the relationship. The husband in the ancient Jewish culture was the head, the authority in the home. As long as the husband is the Law, the wife is subject to live by that authority. But if that husband dies, the wife is free to marry another.

Likewise, my brothers, **you also have died to the law through the body of Christ, so that you may belong to another, to him who has been raised from the dead,** *in order that we may bear fruit for God. For while we were living in the flesh, our sinful passions, aroused by the law, were at work in our members to bear fruit for death.* **But now we are released from the law, having died to that which held us captive, so that we serve in the new way of the Spirit** *and not in the old way of the written code* (Romans 7:4-6).

Paul then explains that we died to the Law when we accepted Christ's death for us. There is an important point of understanding here. When Christ died on the Cross, He

153

didn't simply die for sin, He took the Law with its impossible regulations to the Cross and made it null and void. He abolished the Law in His body. When we try to live according to religious beliefs or a religious culture, we are committing spiritual adultery. We are saying He is not enough. We are saying, "I don't trust that the Cross. Jesus' death for my unrighteousness is insufficient to restore me to Him and the Father." We make the Law alive again. We put ourselves in bondage to the old self again; though we dress it up with our Christian acts and our Christian words, we are not experiencing the fullness of His life. We are not enjoying the fullness of His wonderful *grace.*

When we believe, even in nuance, that we have to act religiously to be in communion with God, we actually are in violation of the covenant relationship. How? Why? Because we are striving, and striving is rooted in fear, not love. When we even subtly slip into a head or heart condition that says, "I must do _____ for God to be okay with me," we are back under the curse. The apostle John speaks clearly into this trap and tells us why:

> *There is* **no fear in love,** *but* **perfect love casts out fear.** *For* **fear has to do with punishment,** *and whoever fears has not been perfected in love* (1 John 4:18).

Here in First John, we see that fear and love can't coexist in the same space. They are polar opposites. Why? Fear is being under the legal judgment of guilt. Love exonerates us from guilt. Either the demonstration of His love at the Cross is our core value, experience, and guide, or it isn't. However, John gives us a very loving and gentle explanation. We have not yet matured to the understanding of His perfect love. The process is not yet completed. The remedy is quite simple.

If this is you, you need to stop the "doing" and pray for greater revelation of God's love for you personally. Our love responders have been interfered with from the brokenness of our sins and the sins of those around us. It is the love of the Father that restores us and brings us to the place of trust and rest. The One who called you out from the grave will never abandon you, reject you, or cast you aside. You can do those things to Him, but He will never do them to you. How illogical would it be for Him to die for you and your sins, then say, "I am done, go back to your sin." Unfortunately, many feel that way and all too often it comes from our religion. Not Christianity, but the way we apply it to our personal religious lives.

The beautiful flipside of all this? He is always near us for communion, deep, intimate conversations and embraces. Jesus says that He came to give us joy, and to give abundantly (see John 10:10). That means He has come to pour love in every expression extravagantly upon us, in us, and through us. What do we need to do to get this joy? Nothing. Well, not exactly nothing. You need only to rest. That's right, rest in the truth that He loves you thoroughly, with all your bumps, bruises, scars, the entire mess you see yourself as—He loves all of you. In resting in His love, you will discover your true self, the one you were created to be.

How do you rest? Resting, especially with the speed of life today, can be difficult. I agree. But there are tools. You can worship, pray, soak, take a walk in nature, go for a drive. What would you do to spend quality time with someone you love? You can read the Bible, pray, do the disciplines. The disciplines aren't bad, unless we think God requires us to do them to have relationship. Then the disciplines become religious works.

I have had many times in my life with Jesus when a discipline was fruitful and intimate—life-giving. Then suddenly it became drab and fruitless. Early on I thought, *What did I do wrong, Lord?* Then, one day, I was with a prophetic friend sharing this struggle. We were driving on a relatively busy North South road where I live on Long Island. We were passing over a cross street. On the front lawn of a corner lot was a hand-painted wooden sign that said, "NO PHONE." We both saw it at the same time but had very different responses. I thought quietly, *That's weird.*

He thought quite loud and demonstratively, "THAT'S IT!"

I looked at him and asked, "What's it?"

He said, "That's it, no phone."

You've lost it, I thought to myself.

But then he said, "That's it, you have no phone. You have been talking to the Lord through the same phone for a long time. He took the phone away. He wants to connect with you in a new way."

My way of relating with my precious Friend, Jesus, had become my method. It was no longer relational; it had become my system. I lost communion because I undervalued the covenant relationship that requires intimacy, pursuit, and passion. Since then, whenever I get too comfortable in a particular way of connecting with Him, He draws me somewhere else. He wants me to know the joy of communion. The communion that is new every day. The first-love communion.

Forever Royalty:
His Bride, Child, Friend, Co-Regent

In closing this chapter, I want to just take a few minutes to unwrap the identities that are given us through this living grace. This grace gift we are given through Christ is not just the gift of new life, eternal life, and forgiveness. It is a working of His life in us that gives us our eternal identities. In those identities we discover our eternal place with Him.

We are forever the bride of Christ. We are the gift of spousal love from the Father for His only begotten and beloved Son. In all that He has made, we alone were created to be His beautiful bride. I have come to believe that a woman on her wedding day is even more beautiful than any previous time.

My wife is beautiful, I am very blessed. She has a beautiful heart and she has natural beauty, as well; anyone who knows her would agree. But that day, when the doors to the church opened and she was standing there. I was stunned at how majestically beautiful she was. I gasped and said to my brother Tony, "She is so beautiful." My response to Patti that day is His response to us, His bride, now and forever. We are and always will be His stunningly beautiful, Father-picked bride. Through the profound power and beauty of His love, all creation will see His great love through us. That power of the only love that can transform ashes to astounding beauty.

We are forever His children. The Father had the Son do all this because He wanted a family that would reflect His countenance, wisdom, and glory as His beloved children. The Godhead is a family of love. Love must multiply, so He created sons and daughters, in Christ, who will love exactly as He loves, revealing yet another aspect of His person and His love.

We will forever be His friends. My wife is my best friend. My sons are also two of my closest friends in life. Family should be friends. I know many times here that is not the case; but in eternity, we will be forever *friends of God*. This relationship is so precious to God. Jesus, on His last night with His disciples, called them friends. He is committed to protecting friendship. His words to Peter at the end of the Gospel of John are at the core a restoration of friendship. When Jesus asks Peter three times, "Do you love Me?" Two of the three times the word for "love" in the Greek is *phileo.* It is the love of brotherly friendship. Jesus was restoring His friend.

We will be co-heirs and co-regents forever. What does this mean? We are forever a royal priesthood. First Peter 2:9 tells us, *"You are...a royal priesthood."* We are royalty in His Kingdom. How can sons and daughters not be royalty? How can the bride of the King not be royalty? We have been born from the blood of our King. We are royalty, created to co-rule and reign in Christ Jesus.

I am going to spend quite a bit of time on this topic in the next chapter. For now, let me just say that this *gift of grace* didn't just save us from sin—it established our place in creation at the side of Jesus forever as His children, His bride, His friends, His family, co-heirs, and co-regents. This is the power of *grace,* the gift of His life in us.

Chapter 7

His Resting Place and Ours

Thus says the Lord: "Heaven is my throne, and the earth is my footstool; **what is the house that you would build for me, and what is the place of my rest?** *All these things my hand has made, and so all these things came to be, declares the Lord. But this is the one to whom I will look: he who is humble and contrite in spirit and trembles at my word"* (Isaiah 66:1-2).

WHEN I READ GENESIS 1, I had very little understanding of the relevance of that chapter beyond the creation narrative. It seemed to me that the whole of the chapter was a beautiful telling of the creation story, demonstrating God's awesome power. It was necessary to be told in order to get to the sixth day, the creation of humankind. You can't just jump to day six, right?

I was able to see how John chapter 1 reveals the creative power, or *fiat*, was the preincarnate Christ, the second Person of the Trinity. But I always had a problem with where it went from there because of one glaring issue, it seemed to me something was already there. I couldn't get around Genesis 1 verse 2 (NIV), *"The earth was formless and empty, darkness was over the surface of the deep, and the Spirit of God was hovering over the waters."* The Hebrew word for earth is *erets.* The meaning of *erets* has a few different applications or usage. It could mean "the whole earth." It could mean simply "earth," the substance of. It can mean "land" or "soil." It can, depending on usage, mean a "territory or country." What it can't mean is "nothing." It can NOT mean nothing is present. Something is already there.

Though I was troubled by this and had some fun conversations over the years about dinosaurs, I would rather not think about it, because if I did, the creation of the material universe's six 24-hour timeframes didn't make sense. I became the ostrich with my head in the sand. Over time I found I wasn't the only one with this question, especially around some Bible college millennials. There was something I was missing. I knew it; it bothered me and I wanted to resolve it. I believed that God created everything, and the part of the story written in Genesis 1 I believed could have been accomplished in six 24-hour days. But concerning the presence of something before, I just resolved to think, *we don't have that part of the story,* and left it alone.

I was in Oklahoma City to speak at the church where my friends Charles and Brian pastor. I was going to speak Sunday, teach at their ministry school Monday evening, then Brian and I were heading to Louisiana to present at a power evangelism conference. Charles told me I needed to read a book by a professor of Old Testament at Wheaton College. While there, I was staying with two of the leaders, Robert and Becky. The next morning, Robert and I had a conversation about Genesis 1, and I mentioned this book. He smiled and said, "You really need to read this book. The author is a scholar in Old Testament and ancient Near East culture. It will blow your mind; you will never read Genesis 1 the same again."

He was right. He handed me a copy and, after just a few minutes, I purchased the Kindle version. The title of the book is *The Lost World of Genesis One,* written by John H. Walton. I just want to give you a very brief summary of what I took away from the book. Then we will put it all together to make beautiful, perfect sense with the name of this chapter.

First, let me say I am not going to cover every detail and supporting information. If you have an interest, I strongly suggest you get the book and read it.

His Cosmic Tabernacle—Our Home

Let's jump in the deep end. Genesis 1 is not the telling of the origins of the material universe. Bam! That is out of the way. Genesis, by tradition, was written by Moses around 1,300 BC. Moses was not writing to well-educated, scientifically Western-thinking men and women. He was writing to shepherds, workers, and the like 1,300 years before Jesus. All the ancient people had a creation story. None had a story that outlined how God, or the gods, created the material world.

For them, the question of who made the heavens and the earth materially was obvious, the gods made it. They were uninterested in how it was done. The science was beyond them. They were interested in how it all was made to work together, function. To the ancients, the gods created the sun so they could have warmth. The earth was created so they could have food, and all these worked together so they could be servants to their gods. They weren't created to be loved or family. They were created to serve the gods; they were no more than slaves at the mercy of the gods. The gods didn't love them; they put up with humans for what we could do for them.

Then comes Abraham and his descendants, who worship one God. This God is very different from all other gods. He loves people. He wants personal relationship with humans. He has a great plan for them. Yes, we serve Him, but He also desires to serve us, through fellowship. He is unlike any other god; the other gods have needs for people to meet. This God has no needs that He demands from us, other than we would love Him as He loves us. This is radically different.

As mentioned before, most ancient Eastern people had an origin story. They didn't need to be told the gods made the material world, they wanted to know how it was all made to work. Why? Because the answer to that question helped them understand their role, why they existed.

Now Moses, inspired by the Lord, writes a different origin story, one that answers the same question. How were things created to work? Walton masterfully unwraps how the first three days are the creation of function, while the second set of three days are the correlating functionaries.

For example, the Bible says about day one: *"Then God said, "Let there be light"; and there was light. And God saw the light, that it was good; and God divided the light from the darkness. God called the light Day, and the darkness He called Night.* **So the evening and the morning were the first day** *"* (Genesis 1:3-5 NKJV). Day one, day and night are spoken into existence, the function is created, the first step for life.

Day four:

> *Then God said, "Let there be lights in the firmament of the heavens to divide the day from the night; and let them be for signs and seasons, and for days and years; and let them be for lights in the firmament of the heavens to give light on the earth"; and it was so. Then God made two great lights: the greater light to rule the day, and the lesser light to rule the night. He made the stars also. God set them in the firmament of the heavens to give light on the earth, and to rule over*

> *the day and over the night, and to divide the light from the darkness. And God saw that it was good. **So the evening and the morning were the fourth day*** (Genesis 1:14-19 NKJV).

So, on day one we have the creation of the function of light and dark, day and night. On day four, the first day on the second set of three days, we have the sun, moon, and stars put in place. These are the functionaries, the elements that rule over the day and night. If you look at the second day (Genesis 1:6-8), God separates the expanse causing waters above and below. The function of atmosphere above and water below. Then on the fifth day (Genesis 1:20-23), He creates the fish for the water below and the birds for above. Day two, we get the function. Day five, the functionaries.

Let's move on to day three (Genesis 1:11-13); here He causes the waters to part, dry land to form, vegetation and fruit to come forth. Everything coming forth has seed within itself to keep reproducing. The function established on day three is land, food from the land, and seed to reproduce of its kind. Day six, God creates man and gives him dominion over all that was made on planet earth. Man is the functionary that maintains earth.

> *God created man in His own image, in the image of God He created him; male and female He created them. Then God blessed them, and God said to them, "Be fruitful and multiply; fill the earth and subdue it; have dominion over the fish of the sea, over the birds of the*

air, and over every living thing that moves on the earth" (Genesis 1:27-28 NKJV).

At the end of this day what was made was declared *"very good"* because His image bearers were now on earth (Genesis 1:31).

Every ancient Near East religion had a creation story that was related to the dwelling place of the gods. The temple of the gods. The most famous is Mount Olympus in Greek mythology. The creation story is also about a tabernacle. But this tabernacle is not made of stone, it is a tabernacle to be made of flesh.

The intention of God in the Bible's creation narrative, His Word, is to communicate with us the how and why of creation. First, He made everything to function, not from the chaos and disorder that existed before Genesis 1:2. He made it all to work in an orderly fashion. We know now that the key to the order for all to function perfectly as intended is love, more specifically His love. Remember, you cannot separate love, light, and life from God. He is all three.

In Acts 17:28 (NKJV), when addressing the Athenians, Paul tells them, *"In Him we live and move and have our being."* When God brings order, He brings Himself. From this we can understand, or at least we should, this planet is to be the cosmic tabernacle of the Living God. Not a tabernacle of earthly stone, but of living stones, sons and daughters indwelt by the Spirit of God to all the fullness of Christ. The Tree of Life is the provision of grace in the Garden, that would have placed in us His life, making us living stones of God. It was and is all about Him having perfect communion with His children. He rested on the seventh day, not because He was tired. He rested because everything was in place, nothing could or can stop it from being fulfilled.

His Throne, His Footstool, His Resting Place

At the beginning of this chapter is Isaiah 66:1 (NKJV): *"Thus says the* Lord*: 'Heaven is My throne, and earth is My footstool. **Where is the house that you will build for Me? And where is the place of My rest?'"** What a profound verse. It is humbling to consider what the Lord is saying here, and it is pointing straight back to Genesis. He made the heavens and the earth. He made these things for Himself. He made us to be His life-bearers in the universe, but our Fall has taken from Him His desired and designed home. We are His resting place.

Back in the early 1990s, Brian Doerksen wrote a beautiful worship song called, "Resting Place." It takes Isaiah 66:1 with God singing and then adds a response from the worshipper:

Heaven is My throne
And earth is My footstool

Where is the house you will build for Me?
Whom of you will hear the cry of My heart
Where will my resting place be?
Here oh Lord have I prepared for You a home
Long have I desired for You to dwell
Here oh Lord have I prepared a resting place
Here oh Lord I wait for You alone.

This is the fruition of God's heart and purpose for creating humankind. This should be the response of every believer: "Here, Lord, rest in me." Even as we are to rest in Him, His desire and purpose for us is that He would find eternal rest within His creation—in you and me, sons and daughters, His friends and His bride.

This is amazing to consider and there are some incredible statements made in Scripture.

Empowered to Rule and Reign

When I was in South Africa in June 2018, I was in a meeting with some leaders in Jeffery's Bay. During worship, one of the leaders attending spoke up and said that she was feeling pressed from the Holy Spirit to read from Isaiah 9:6 (NIV): *"For to us a child is born, to us a son is given, and **the government will be on his shoulders**, and he will be called*

Wonderful Counselor, Mighty God, Everlasting Father, Prince of Peace." As soon as she read it, I heard Holy Spirit speak in my heart, "Where are the shoulders?" Immediately I knew He was referring to the Body of Christ. That evening I was told I was going to speak the next morning. I want to unwrap a bit of that teaching here.

I started that next morning by sharing what had happened the night before. How I heard the Lord call my attention to the phrase, *"and the government will be on his shoulders."* I asked, "Where are your shoulders?" I answered for them, "Right below your head." Christ is the Head and we are the Body.

I then went to Genesis, the beginning, *"be fruitful, multiply and take dominion."* That is a rulership statement. In the beginning we were to rule over the planet, that lordship was taken by satan, the usurper. Jesus came in the flesh to take back the authority. He did this as a man. Yes, He is God. He is fully God and He is fully man. What He did while here in the flesh was as a man, *"the firstborn among many brothers and sisters"* (Romans 8:29 NIV). The prototype of those who were to follow. He had to do this so that He would forever be first among all others. Lord of all. But He has given us His Spirit to bring us by His grace, His life working in us, that we would be what He created us to be. The kings that would exercise His dominion and authority on earth.

Calling ourselves kings may seem a bit arrogant, except the Scripture says that we are kings. In Revelation 1:5-6 many Bibles say, *"...To him who loves us and has freed us from our sins by his blood and **made us a kingdom**, priests to his God and*

Father...." The problem with this is that the Greek doesn't say "kingdom," it says "kings," which makes more grammatical sense. In this case, the New King James Version is the correct translation, *"To Him who loved us and washed us from our sins in His own blood, and **has made us kings** and priests to His God and Father...."* One of the titles of Jesus is King of kings. We are the kings, lowercase k, to His King, uppercase K. But nonetheless, we are kings. We have been commissioned to exercise His justice, His government.

Romans 16:20 tells us, *"The God of peace will soon crush Satan under your feet."* This is a reference to authority. In Genesis 3:15, we are told the curse of the serpent is enmity between the woman and the snake. Her offspring will bruise the head of the serpent, that is authority; but the serpent will bruise the heel, that is the walk. Jesus is the One who crushed satan's authority when He descended to Hades and took back the keys over death. But, because we were made to be His dwelling, He desires that we get the authority that was taken when we were immature.

Jesus is going to crush satan under the feet of His children, His bride. This speaks into the restoration of authority. We have been empowered to execute the authority of Heaven here on earth. We do this by healing the sick, raising the dead, and casting out demons. Every time we do, Heaven invades earth. Ultimately, as we are demonstrating the power of the Kingdom, souls are saved by the proclamation of the Gospel and the Kingdom expands. We are being fruitful, multiplying, and subduing.

Most Western believers seem to think that the Church is in trouble. That may be in part because we tend to think we are the world. However, the truth couldn't be further from this assessment. There are more believers on the planet today than ever before. There are more supernatural healings than ever before. More demons are getting cast out than ever before.

I have a friend; he is a dangerous son of God. He goes into some of the scariest places in the world. He wants to see hundreds of thousands, even millions of Muslims come to the saving knowledge of Jesus. He recently told me that on his most recent trip, as best as they could count, between 25,000 and 30,000 Muslims gave their lives to the Lord in just ten days. I have heard from friends similar stories in China. In three weeks in South Africa, in meetings no larger than 200 and the vast majority out in the streets, we had well over 500 healed, and over 300 give their lives to Jesus, of which at least one-third were Muslim. This is just a handful of believers going about their daily business and doing what Jesus did. That is the Kingdom.

This is the clear evidence that we have been empowered by the grace of His life in us to exercise His authority, release His Kingdom, and release His government. That tells me, we were created, born again, and filled with the Spirit of God, at least in part, to rule in Christ.

We are His resting place and His tabernacle. In the not-too-distant future, the fullness of this truth will be fully realized when He returns for His bride and His army of lovers. His grace is more than favor alone. It is favor in that we are His prize, His treasure—so it is favor like my wife has favor with me because I adore her. It has nothing to do with not deserving, and everything to do with who He created us to be. You are the most valuable, most treasured and precious possession of God.

Chapter 8

God Is Always Good

On the other hand, we know that if there does exist an absolute goodness it must hate most of what we do. That is the terrible fix we are in. ...We cannot do without it, and we cannot do with it. God is the only comfort; He is also the supreme terror: the thing we most need and the thing we most want to hide from. He is our only possible-ally, and we have made ourselves His enemies. Some people talk as if meeting the gaze of absolute goodness would be fun. They need to think again. They are still only playing with religion. Goodness is either the great safety or the great danger–according to the way you react to it. And we have reacted the wrong way.

–C.S. Lewis

IF WE ARE TO UNDERSTAND grace in all its beauty and power, we need to understand what it means when Jesus says only God is good. Within His nature, the very essence of God is perfect goodness. From God's perfect goodness comes the life of Holy Spirit empowering us, sustaining us, and raising us up as His image bearers.

> *Then they brought little children to Him, that He might touch them; but the disciples rebuked those who brought them. But when Jesus saw it, He was greatly displeased and said to them, "Let the little children come to Me, and do not forbid them; for of such is the kingdom of God. Assuredly, I say to you, whoever does not receive the kingdom of God as a little child will by no means enter it." And He took them up in His arms, laid His hands on them, and blessed them. Now as He was going out on the road, one came running, knelt before Him, and asked Him, "Good Teacher, what shall I do that I may inherit eternal life?" So Jesus said to him, "Why do you call Me good?* **No one is good but One, that is, God** (Mark 10:13-18 NKJV).

We see here the Man, Jesus. He is not speaking from His divinity but from His humanity, asking this man, "Why do you call Me good?" He is stating, whether they realize it or not, that humanity is not the measure of good. Jesus is causing us to reevaluate how we define what is good or who is good. It's important to understand this distinction.

All too often we judge God based on what we think He should be. We end up judging Him on our criteria. He is telling the onlookers, if you are to understand what is good, you need to know what makes God good. We can never judge or evaluate what is good by looking at a person's behavior because we all define good differently, and generally God is not our standard. Jesus is telling us God alone is the measure of what is good.

Defining Good

The word Mark uses here for *good* is *agathós*. Strong's Concordance tells us it means "inherently (intrinsically) *good*; as to the believer, (*agathós*) describes what *originates from God* and is *empowered* by Him in their life, through faith." When we consider grace as the empowerment of God, or the life and power of Holy Spirit working in all the wonderful ways of His grace, we can see it comes from an intrinsically "Good God."

We can do good things, but that does not make us good. Jesus is pulling the children close, blessing them, probably healing people, and this man calls Him "Good Teacher." Jesus was the greatest teacher. I have had really good teachers in my life and some not-so-good teachers in my life. Jesus is seizing the opportunity to bring the intrinsic good that is in God into the conversation. He wants to lift our eyes up to the One who is perfect in goodness and help us understand He is the goal. As image bearers, we are to be and are becoming the very presence of the Good God to the world around us. Therefore, no one can model what is good, only God can.

So, what makes God good? Here are just a few qualities among many more:

- God's love is sacrificial.
- He is never self-seeking.
- He is always patient and kind.
- Although God is in control, He never controls us.
- He is slow to anger and quick to embrace.
- His love is not fickle; God is always willing to take the first step.
- He is ever hopeful.
- God is always faithful.
- He never fails to pursue us, regardless of our sin.
- He loves us perfectly.
- There is no fear in God.
- His generosity is unmatched.

In the end, God loves every person with an unshakeable and unquenchable love. God is not simply a loving person, He is and always has been the very essence of perfect love in action. He is the substance of love; and whenever you see someone loving others well, sacrificially and generously, you see God revealed.

I love Psalm 139; it is one of the most beautiful psalms in Scripture. It captures the tenacity of God's love and goodness toward us. Notice how the writer speaks of the hand of God in verse 10.

Where shall I go from your Spirit? Or where shall I flee from your presence? If I ascend to heaven, you are there! If I make my bed in Sheol, you are there! If I take the wings of the morning and dwell in the uttermost parts of the sea, even there your hand shall lead me, and your right hand shall hold me (Psalm 139:7-10).

This psalm of David's is so revealing of God's heart, His goodness in pursuing a son who had sinned. David is calling attention to the omniscience of God. Whether David has done something wrong, is facing some turmoil, or has sinned, this psalm tells us God is always present and ready to take us into His loving embrace and bring us through whatever trial or pain we are living in, even when we want to hide. There is no place we can go to escape God and this includes when we have sinned. The Lord responds by leading us by His hand, holding us close.

I find it amazing that God, our Father, even in our worst times, operates out of His goodness with love to redirect us and to hold us. I never stop being awestruck by the goodness of His love. This psalm perfectly captures why God is good.

Going back to Mark 10, we can see this man, this seeker, was clearly pursuing God—but under a religious culture. He didn't know what had to be done to receive eternal life with God in Heaven. He is of the belief that there is something he has to do, something perhaps he has not and is not presently doing. This is causing him some level of concern, enough to call out and ask his question. He observes the actions and behavior of Jesus and decides Jesus is good. Surely no one would argue against that point. Jesus however sees a teaching opportunity, a very important one. He points us to our process of determining what is good.

Our reasoning is based on observations of peoples' behavior. We draw our conclusions of who is good and who is not based on the actions we can see. When we apply this kind of thinking to God, along with a belief system that teaches God is in complete control and therefore everything that happens is caused by God, we can get in trouble in our heart and mind. Why? The inevitable outcome is that when bad things happen, we put that on God, which immediately causes conflict in our hearts—or we go to the place of ignorant bliss. We don't want to wrestle through the way we process, because we have been taught that God is in control.

We believe being in control means complete control of everything and everyone. This way of thinking demonstrates that we've been taught that God is controlling. Being in control and being controlling are not the same thing. Equally problematic with this line of thinking is it allows satan to slip through the cracks scot-free of any responsibility. In the extreme, this thinking could even remove any individual responsibility for our own responses and actions. Comedian Flip Wilson had a popular weekly comedy show. One of his characters was named Geraldine. Geraldine was always getting herself into situations and would explain herself out of it by saying "The devil made me do it." The skits were funny and demonstrated through humor how we avoid taking responsibility for our poor choices. As well as the idea that God in His control allows people to not take responsibility for their own choices.

Seeing God in this way, the cause of everything that happens, leads us to a place where we can observe going-ons in the world and question, "If God is good, then why…?" We say things like, "If God is good why did so-and-so die so young," or, "If God is good, why would this catastrophe happen and so many innocent people died," or, "If God is good, why would He allow this person to come into leadership?" These are all valid questions and sometimes come from deep pain, compassion, and or a hatred for injustices, either to ourselves or to others. But most often these situations we put on God are *not* God. Freewill has to be exercised, responsibility for choices taken, and maturity in wisdom grown if we are to become the image of God we are created to be.

He Is in Control—But He Is *Not* Controlling

What is the problem with this way of thinking? It's dangerous because it positions us to judge God. The enemy's primary weapons are to cause us to question our identity as His children or to question God's integrity, His goodness toward us. Many believers have not been properly taught what makes God good, so they actually end up judging Him when things don't go their way. If our theology says God is in complete control and everything that happens is God's will, legitimate questions are asked. Questions that can cause turmoil in our souls, because we don't understand the relationship between the goodness of God and His control. However, the truth is God is not controlling and yet still maintains control, working everything for His good plan for us.

When we think that being in control is the same as controlling, we get into trouble. To be controlling means to exert power over a people's freewill, to cause them to do something they would not do otherwise. For instance, a married couple may have one person who is controlling and exerts his or her will on the spouse to benefit only his or her own interests. This is the typical motivation behind witchcraft. When we think of witchcraft, we generally think of dark figures speaking incantations or doing other things to cause someone harm or to gain control over them. We've all read fairytales or seen movies about the lovestruck guy or girl who buys a love potion so the person they are enamored with will love them. That's witchcraft.

When we use fear, control, and/or manipulation that takes a people's right to choose away, exerting control of them, that's a form of witchcraft. Religion, when taken too far, can manifest in controlling people, often through fear, which damages the hearts of people. When we think God is in control, we're not saying God is controlling—He is not making people do things they wouldn't otherwise do. If He were, that would be manipulation, exerting control for His own purposes; that is not love, and that is not the meaning of being in control.

What does it mean to say God is in control but is not controlling? It simply means God is still working in partnership with those people who choose Him, to bring a good result forth. When we are in that type of synergistic relationship, Jesus works everything together for our good. He always brings beauty from ashes when we live in partnership with Him. Nothing is lost that cannot be restored because He is in control.

This is a discussion that has been going on forever. I agree, for the most part, with the Eastern Orthodox view, which says that the work of salvation, and even living out our faith in victory, is a synergistic relationship. God offers the choice, the opportunities to choose what is good, and humans exercising our freewill must respond. Eastern Orthodox offers "the parable of a drowning man" to illustrate the teaching of synergy: God, from a ship, throws a rope to a drowning man; and if the man wants to be saved, he must hold on tightly to the rope being safely pulled up and placed on the deck. This parable explains salvation is both a gift from God and a response from individuals. We cannot save ourselves, we must co-work (synergo) with God in the process of salvation. God initiates the invitation; the invitation requires people to respond freely.

The Goodness of God
Is Not Conditional, It Is Purposeful

I have done some work pressing into what "God is good" means. I discovered something very interesting. In the vast majority of Scripture speaking into God as good, almost all point to His generosity as being the indicator of His goodness. I find this fascinating. God is good in large part because of His commitment to and joy in being generous to His creation. When Jesus is teaching the Sermon on the Mount, in Matthew chapter 5, He points to God's goodness. If we don't pay attention we can easily miss it.

> *You have heard that it was said, "Love your neighbor and hate your enemy."* **But I tell you, love your enemies and pray for those who persecute you, that you may be children of your Father in heaven.** **He causes his sun to rise on the evil and the good, and sends rain on the righteous and the unrighteous.** *If you love those who love you, what reward will you get? Are not even the tax collectors doing that? And if you greet only your own people, what are you doing more than others? Do not even pagans do that?* **Be perfect, therefore, as your heavenly Father is perfect** (Matthew 5:43-48 NIV).

Jesus is pointing to the unconditional generosity in the Father's heart. His love is demonstrated through His generosity. He doesn't love, provide, or care for only those people who love or like Him; no, He is generous to everyone. He is generous to both the evil and good, the righteous and unrighteous. Jesus raises the bar by challenging us to do the same: "*Be perfect, therefore, as your heavenly Father is perfect.*" Jesus is not pointing to behaving perfectly. He is calling us upward to love maturely just like our heavenly Father, generosity plays a huge part in demonstrating love maturely, unselfishly, and revealing our God.

What does all this have to do with redefining grace? Remember the central point of this book is that the gift of grace is Holy Spirit living in you. I called it the life of the Spirit in us or living by the Spirit. Grace is the active working of Spirit life in us. When we look at the expressions of grace in Scripture, we see:

- Saving Grace
- Empowering Grace
- Sustaining Grace
- Strengthening Grace

All of these expressions of grace are simply telling us what power is active situationally to help His children. But all of those things are the work of the Spirit. Grace is simply a term to describe the life of Holy Spirit in you working synergistically to transform you into the image of God. The "good and generous gift of God to us" is His Spirit living in us. All the activities of what we call grace are the result of living in loving communion with the Spirit of God in us.

As stated previously, the definition of grace as God's unmerited favor is weak. From the very beginning the plan was for His Spirit to live in you, and for you and Holy Spirit to become one. If my plan for one of my sons, from before they were even born, was to give them the family business, when the day comes for them to receive it, unmerited gift is such a poor perspective, because I determined the business was theirs from the beginning, before they could have done anything good or bad.

God determined from before the beginning to make you His dwelling place by His Spirit. All provision for every part of your being was going to always be provided by His Spirit living in you. Holy Spirit *is* the grace of God. That is why grace after grace abounds to you, because the Source of grace lives *in* you. The goodness of God is most greatly seen in the gift He gives which is Himself, living in the bond of love within you. Grace is simply the word chosen to describe the life of Holy Spirit in us. Jesus said, *"I am the way"*: love. *"I am the truth"*: the reality you live from. *"I am the life"*: His Spirit lives in you. Can anything be more intimate? Can anything be more powerful? Can anything be more wonderful or beautiful? NO!

In closing this chapter, and coming to the close of our journey together, I would like you to consider something Irenaeus said about us. We, the offspring of God, are to become deified in nature, as He is deified in essence. What does that mean? While God is God in His very essence, His beingness, we are becoming like Him in our nature. Our nature, character, wisdom, love, thoughts, and emotions will be as His. That is the most beautiful kindness revealing why God alone is good.

Chapter 9

Living the Life
of the Spirit

In the beginning, man's spirit was the dominant force in the world. When he sinned, his mind became dominant. Sin dethroned the spirit and crowned the intellect. But grace is restoring the spirit to its place of dominion. When man comes to realize this, he will live in the realm of the supernatural without effort.

–John G. Lake

WE'VE COVERED A LOT OF GROUND in these pages. We discussed theology, history, grace in the Old Testament, grace in the New Testament, and more. This is all just information if you can't take hold of the value of this concept of grace actually being the Life of Holy Spirit in you. I don't want to simply give you information, no matter how thought provoking or powerful. If it doesn't move you along the road into deeper places of His love and transformation, what was the point?

Let's review, readdress, and reveal some of the practical points, takeaways, and tools to fully take hold of *Redefining Grace*. There is power, freedom, and joy in grasping hold of this. When I think of grace now, it isn't a power I am given when I need something. It is the by-product of intimate *communion* with the Spirit of God who lives in me. It isn't something I ask for in times of need, it is His presence meeting all my needs. Grace is not a gift like a great Swiss army knife with something for every situation. No, the solution in every situation is God Himself who lives in us. Holy Spirit is *the* beautiful and amazing Grace.

The gifts of the Spirit are simply what the Life of the Spirit does. He heals through us because He is the Healer. He speaks prophecy through us because He is the Message and the Messenger. He makes known the revelatory gifts because He is the Spirit of wisdom and truth. He works miracles because He is the Superior Reality that invades earth. He is the Gift of Faith, because all things are possible with Him. Holy Spirit is the omnipresent, omniscient, omnipotent One and He lives in you and me. When I meditate on that, it is an awe-inspiring, terrifyingly beautiful truth. Oh, the depths of perfect love that can live in the brokenness of humanity and yet still call us beloved. Oh, the everlasting grace present before the foundation of the world and will still be there when all things are made new.

What Does it All Mean
This Side of Heaven?

The truth is this, humankind has never lost the influence of dominion over the planet. From the beginning we were given lordship over the earth. We were made to execute that lordship in a place of fellowship with God. In fact, our lordship requires fellowship and communion with the holy God because we were made to be His image bearers, to grow in His nature until we are filled to His fullness. The problem came when we rejected God through the seduction of satan, which was to have our own way. In that rebellion, the enemy began to mold us in his own image of fear. Through satan's influence and the selfish, self-centered nature we took, we placed ourselves at the center of everything and molded the entire planet in our image, and so all suffered and still suffers. This is why Paul writes in Romans:

> *For the creation waits in eager expectation for the children of God to be revealed. For the creation was subjected to frustration, not by its own choice, but by the will of the one who subjected it, in hope that the creation itself will be liberated from its bondage to decay and brought into the freedom and glory of the children of God. We know that the whole creation has been groaning as in the pains of childbirth right up to the present time. Not only so, but we ourselves, who have the firstfruits of the Spirit, groan inwardly as we wait*

> *eagerly for our adoption to sonship, the redemption of
> our bodies* (Romans 8:19-23 NIV).

We see here there is even a synergistic relationship between
the material creation, specifically earth, and the children of
God. All the children of God, male and female. The word
used for sonship here can also be interpreted *offspring.* As we
go, so goes this planet. When we pray, "Let it be on earth as
in Heaven," it is important that we understand the coming
of Heaven manifesting on earth is, in part, a response to His
children being transformed into His family and His image
and nature. Notice it doesn't say creation is waiting for Jesus
to come back, though I wholeheartedly await the return of
our King, Jesus. But it does say, *"creation waits with eager long-
ing for the children of God to be revealed."*

I believe it is important for us to start to fully take hold of
the reality that the grace of God is the gift of Jesus for salvation—but equally important is the gift of the Life of Holy
Spirit in us, teaching us, transforming us in loving communion. As we yield to the intimacy and power of this union,
not simply the theology of grace, we start to become what
Irenaeus spoke of, deified in nature—simply meaning that
we are becoming like Him in our hearts, minds, and soul in
the way we live, love, and engage the world around us. That
is when Heaven will come to earth. When we embrace the
fullness of this truth, Heaven will manifest through us and
in us. The world will see in His family the reality of Heaven;
and when Jesus returns, it will be seen in its fullness. But for

now, we must do our part to embrace Holy Spirit, fully surrendering ourselves to His love.

How Do We Live in His Reality?

Living in His reality is not easy, but it isn't hard either.
One of the main points of this book is that grace isn't something you necessarily have to ask for—the Spirit of Life is in
you. We simply need to intentionally acknowledge His presence in us, yield to Him, and spend time with Holy Spirit in
prayer, worship, meditation, contemplation, and, of course,
His Word, the Bible. But it has to be more than simply time
spent, it must be with the understanding of intimate communion with Holy Spirit. All too often when we pray and
worship, we see God as up there hopefully coming down to
us. The truth is He isn't up there, He is inside you and all
around you.

When we worship, we aren't asking God to come down
from some a high place; rather, ask Him to enter into our
presence and bring us into His presence. Heaven is all
around us, only separated by a veil of fear and lies. Holy
Spirit is in you, carrying the very presence of Heaven inside
you just waiting to flow out of you. If the Lord is all around
us, then Heaven is actually all around us as well. If Holy
Spirit is in us, then we have Heaven in us. The question is,
what is our reality?

When Jesus says in John 14:6, *"I am the truth,"* He was telling those listening, *"I am reality."* The Greek word for *truth* is *alitheia*. This word translated in English as "truth" in Greek is "reality." He is telling us, when we see Him, we see what is eternal, He is our reality. So, we fix our eyes on Jesus. He wants to be more real to us than the things we are told are real. For instance, the media is all about programing us toward fear. Why? Because fear keeps you connected more than love. When we are afraid, we become fixated with what we fear, making that fear the reality we live from. Jesus is saying, "Fix your eyes on Me, I overcome all that is false, all illusion."

To live in this reality, we must focus our hearts and minds on Jesus. How do we do that? Being in the Word, prayer, and worship are obvious. Also, being in good, healthy community—walking together in love and sincere, authentic honor, while giving Holy Spirit room to engage through healing, words of knowledge, prophecy, but most importantly intimate, wholehearted, Presence-driven worship of Father, Son, and Holy Spirit. Build redemptive relationships with people who are safe. Invest in developing relationships where you are not only intimate and transparent, but also vulnerable.

We can be intimate, and we can even let people see through the window of our hearts, but vulnerability requires the risk of allowing people who love you speak into you. Find spiritual fathers and mothers to mentor you. I say fathers and mothers and not simply pastors or leaders because it's not the title that makes you wise, sensitive, or safe. Look for those who are willing to invest relationally into you, not because of your skills, gifts, or potential. Fathers and mothers are those who have paid the price to gain godly wisdom; they are humble, and genuine lovers of people. They are worth their weight in gold.

Cultivate a moment-by-moment lifestyle with God. I try to talk to Him throughout the day. Cultivate an awareness that He is always right by your side, in every moment of every day. Pursue personal renewal, take care of your inner life with Him. While you can, and should, cultivate your secret place with Him, He always has access to all your secrets, so be relationally authentic with Holy Spirit. There is nothing but love and acceptance in Him.

Remember you are in process, transformation doesn't happen overnight; you are on a journey of Christ discovery. This journey is going to ultimately bring you to the place where you will be like Him, so don't give any room for shame, insecurity, or unforgiveness; let all of those things go as fast as you can and jump into the arms of Abba, your heavenly Father.

Understanding now that grace is simply a word to describe the Life of Holy Spirit in you, devote yourself to your transformation and be with people who obviously want to partner with you and God on your behalf. You need them at relational, brother-sister and father-mother levels. Being transformed through the gift of grace, the Spirit of Life in you, happens best in healthy, loving, emotionally healthy community.

Being Light Bearers to a World in Darkness

When I think of being a light bearer, I go back again to the words of Jesus in John 14. In fact, all of John's writings speak into the topic of being a light bearer to a dark world. John unwraps in His Gospel and in First John an amazing truth. In John's Gospel Jesus says, *"I am the way, the truth and the life."* Paralleling that understanding in First John, John says, God is love and God is light.

So, the essence of God comes to these three things:

1. *God is love.* When Jesus says, "Be perfect as My heavenly Father is perfect," He means demonstrate love generously, in a mature manner, *holding nothing back* because of who people are. Love everyone. You can do that when you yield to Holy Spirit, because He is the Spirit of love and will empower you to love as you surrender.

2. Love releases *God's light.* The light of His love is holding all things together and the God who is light lives in you.

3. Finally, *God is life,* not simply heart-pumping life, but life for the soul to live joyfully, purposefully,

and abundantly. You have in you the God who is love, light, and life. When you demonstrate those attributes with compassion, kindness, and action, His light comes through. Just risk to go love someone. I have seen lives touched in this way through healing, words of knowledge, and even godly wisdom in grocery stores, coffee shops, restaurants, on the streets, even at drive-thru restaurant windows. Sometimes it is a profound healing, other times it is a kind and loving word into a person's heart. God's love, light, and life shine light into darkness.

My good friend, Brian Blount, likes to say, "When you walk out the door to touch people with the power and love of Jesus, you have already succeeded." So, in all these things, risk loving, demonstrate His love and power. When you do that, you will shine His light into the darkness almost effortlessly.

Tearing Down Strongholds

The most significant barrier to allowing the power and life of Holy Spirit to flow from you, transforming you and touching those around you, are strongholds. Strongholds are lies you bought into that build into you negative self-talk, poor identity, and empowered lies that become your paradigm for relationships and for the world you live in. Strongholds are built into us over a lifetime through hurt, rejection, trauma, lost love, various fears, etc. It starts to define who you are and, in time, imprisons you as a helpless and hopeless captive.

Not all people carry strongholds that lead them into the darkest places, but most have agreed with a lie that speaks into them an identity contrary to God's. For instance, people who have had lots of rejection in life will perceive all relationships as risky, with the expectation of getting rejected over and over again. Often when they get rejected, they think, "Here we go again...," but often it is because they're incorrectly interpreting an event or words as rejection. Kind of like a self-fulfilling prophecy.

We overcome these things by speaking truth to ourselves, by asking Holy Spirit to bring His life and His truth into our hearts and minds. When those lies rise up in us, we simply say no and we ask Holy Spirit to give us more of His life, light, and a greater revelation of His love. The Spirit living in you is the power to overcome these lies. He is the grace in your life to overcome all the works of the enemy. Remember, God is in particular these three things: 1) He is perfect Love; 2) He is fullness of Life; and 3) He is Light and Truth.

Strongholds always attack these areas of our soul: First, our capacity to fully love or be loved. Secondly, our ability to live a good and godly life filled with joy, hope, and glorious expectations. Finally, and perhaps most importantly, strongholds keep you from knowing truth, the truth of who God is and the truth of who you are to Him. This is not a battle that can be won solely by declaring over yourself. All too often this is a way by works and not by grace.

You overcome strongholds through intimacy, vulnerability, and obedience to the Lord. Intimacy with Holy Spirit is to engage in love at all costs. Vulnerability means to embrace a commitment that says, "Search me and know me" (see Psalm 139:1). A commitment to let go of our own way and take hold of His.

Finally, be obedient in the process. I have never seen someone set free from strongholds without committing to do as asked without question. In my own battle with strongholds there were battles of trusting the Lord or not trusting. He required me to be obedient and take hold of truth even if it hurt or meant letting go of something or someone I had affection for but kept me bound in a lie. Obedience requires trust and trust is only trust when we step into an unknown place. Thankfully, we have His Spirit in us, drawing us closer and beckoning us to let go of those things that will not bring life.

It is important to note, that while grace is ever-present in the Spirit, even here we have freewill to take hold of grace or not. Holy Spirit is living in you and is ever-present to provide whatever is needed in a given situation, but generally will not push His way on us. Though there have been times the Lord moved sovereignly in my life, generally it is an invitation. An invitation to enter into the most beautiful, powerful, amazing relationship.

To live by the Spirit is to face life fearlessly knowing whatever comes your way, He will always bring something good. It is to live a life full of hope because the God of Hope lives in you. It is to live in peace, because the Spirit of Peace saturates you. You only need to slow down, *selah,* take a breath and invite Him to rise up in you—there He will be, leading you, comforting you, encouraging you, and empowering you. The living grace of God in you.

All in all, I hope you will live from the place of understanding grace is not something you get in times of need, but is the life of Holy Spirit rising up from inside you when you need His strength, guidance, and power. Remember, intimate relationship, authentic fellowship, and passion is what He wants. Grace for the believer is best activated through a loving relationship with the Lord.

The Romance and the Lovers Dance

God created things which had free will. That means creatures which can go wrong or right. Some people think they can imagine a creature which was free but had no possibility of going wrong, but I can't. **If a thing is free to be good, it's also free to be bad.** *...Why, then, did God give them free will?* **Because free will, though it makes evil possible, is also the that only thing makes possible any love or goodness or joy worth having.** *...The happiness which God designs for His higher creatures is the happiness of being freely, voluntarily united to Him and to each other in an ecstasy of love and delight compared with which the most rapturous love between a man and a woman on this earth is mere milk and water. And for that they've got to be free.*

–C.S. Lewis, Mere Christianity

I LOVE THIS C.S. LEWIS QUOTE. The brilliance of it captures the very heart of God and speaks into the understanding of grace I have been sharing. I sincerely do not understand the position of freewill violating God's sovereignty. Why would our Sovereign God, given capacity to freely choose, limit His sovereignty? If in His sovereign plan He chose for humanity to have freedom of choice for His purpose to be realized, does it make Him less sovereign? Not at all! Does our freewill mean God doesn't, at times, move sovereignly? Absolutely not, He is still Lord.

Scripture is filled with paradox and mystery. Our reasoning process, particularly in the West, likes nice, neat, lineal, it-all-makes-perfect-sense conclusions. What I have discovered is an almost endless number of paradoxical words in Scripture.

God is perfect in love. His lovingkindness endures forever. He loves mercy. So many beautiful things about Him. But then there's also things like wrath, rage, indignation, etc. There are warnings to avoid His judgment. All too often I hear preachers overly focused on one of the extremes. They preach fire and brimstone messages to an extreme, while others preach love that is equal in its extreme.

God is love, so you don't ever have to worry about His anger. God isn't angry. I agree the nature of God is not anger—He is love. But if you continually violate love, He can get pretty ticked off. You cannot have perfect love and, when that love is violated, not experience righteous anger. It is important that we find balance learning to live in the tension, while at the same time accepting that we aren't going to have all the answers. I am alright with that, because I know Him and perhaps most importantly, I trust Him.

In Chapter 3, I wrote about a Christmas present and the need to know the function or purpose of a gift. Knowing its function is critical, both in knowing what you can do with it and the personal value you can place on it, based on its usefulness to you specifically. For instance, if someone gave me a little garden rake, it wouldn't be held in high esteem for me. I grew up as my mom's personal landscaper; though I really was happy to serve her, I took very little joy in it. Hence, a nice garden utensil wouldn't be of much value for me. But for my wife, Patti, she'd love it; she enjoys tinkering in the garden, and in her flowerpots of all kinds. Gardening gives her life; she finds peace when she is planting flowers. As you can see, function is important.

What does this have to do with grace, freewill, and the sovereignty of God? It has a lot to do with all three. For us to take hold of the full meaning and purpose of what we call grace, we have to first understand and take hold of God's big purpose for humankind. All too often we limit the beauty of why God made us, containing it within religious language rooted in fear. We need to be willing to explore the beauty of God with great freedom.

From my experience, many of my brothers and sisters in Christ are so bound up in the fear of falling or failing. So many miss out on the beauty and mystery of walking with the Master, our Bridegroom and Lord. If you are afraid to make a mistake, relating to the extreme you just read about, living in unhealthy fear of the Lord, I hope you will find the courage to risk and reach out and discover Christ more fully. There is so much fear in the Church. So many are believing more in the enemy's capacity to deceive, as opposed to the Lord's capacity to keep us near. Remember, for deception to work, your agreement is necessary.

Many years ago, I was under a controlling leadership structure. I was always in fear of getting it wrong. I lived not from a place of expectancy or joy, but from a place of insecurity and anxiety. In prayer one day toward the end of my time there, the Lord gave me a vision. I was a strong, young stallion in a corral located in horse country. Something you might see in Kentucky. I could see other corrals in a maze of perfectly groomed and maintained fence-lined paths. Jesus came into my corral; as He drew closer to me, I experienced great excitement, expectation, and joy. He touched me and I immediately was at peace. I expected Him to bridle me and take me for a run; but instead, He draped a rope around my neck and gently led me out from the corral. He led me through the fence-lined maze, smiling at me as we walked.

Finally, we came to a gate. Beyond the gate was a beautiful landscape of rolling hills, trees, and a large creek flowing down into the plains below. He opened the gate and I froze. I had never been out of the safety of my corral. There was no fear there, and no risk. I was content in my small world without risk. But this was completely different. If He rode me, I would venture out. But no way would I go out on my own.

I looked at Him, terrified of the open field. He said, "Go, run free, I made you for this." I stayed frozen in place. I finally got the courage to speak, "Lord, I don't know where the boundaries are. I might go too far and either fall or get lost. I don't want to get lost or risk losing You." Jesus then challenged me and helped me realize the boundaries of my safe corral were actually fences built from fear. They weren't boundaries, but the walls of my own prison. They were built from a religious culture built around fear and control.

Jesus said, "I made you to run free. You need to trust My love and purpose for you. Trust Me; if you go too far, I will be there to bring you back to Me. I will never be far from you." I became aware that His love for me was more powerful than my fear. I was immediately free to join Him in pursuing love more fully, and I began to discover my voice, empowered to dream with Jesus. This is the by-product of the love-filled grace that brings new life. He has kept His word that day to me for more than twenty years.

On the other hand, the other extreme, the one that says God doesn't get angry, can be a bit out of balance as well. Let me say I tend to lean or err in this direction, too. If I am going to err, I want to err on the side of love—not fear or control. However, it is important not to forget He is the holy God and the righteous Judge. Hell is a real place and there are those who will choose against Him. Let's not forget to challenge in love and preach the whole Scripture.

To paraphrase the *Chronicles of Narnia,* "Safe? Aslan isn't safe, but He is good. He is the King I tell you." Scriptures tell us there is a wrath of God and makes clear we don't want to take it lightly. Personally, I believe His wrath is against satan and sin, so when His wrath comes to eradicate sin from creation, those not covered by His blood will fall under His wrath against sin.

This is not a message we like to share, and I don't believe it is one we should talk about excessively, as it tends to bring fear. We do, however, need to not forget; pastors and teachers should not ignore this reality. I am stunned by how many young people don't believe in hell or the final judgment. Perhaps in our desire to reveal our Father's love, we have forgotten to bring it all into balance with the truth of His sovereign lordship.

My concern is this perspective may bring some people to a place where grace, the power of His life working in us, is not fully effective, because it seems purity and godliness is not hotly pursued. Instead there is a pursuit of experiences, that for some takes the place of true discipleship. Because we have freewill, we can choose to position ourselves to receive grace upon grace, life and more life, or not. Let's choose obedience with grace and walk in true discipleship. The Spirit in you is committed to bring you life when you say, "Yes, Lord," especially to His leading you away from unrighteousness.

Freewill Means Forever Free in His Love

We need to answer some "why" questions in order to fully understand how grace is the bridge between or glue that holds sovereignty and freewill together. Some questions we have already discussed, but let's readdress them here to wrap up everything.

Why did God create? I am not going to pretend to have all the answers to this God-sized question. Only He knows all of His reasons. But the Bible does give us good insight. Of course, Genesis 1 says, *"In the beginning God created...."* However, my favorite verse to demonstrate God's creativeness is Ephesians 2:10: *"For we are his workmanship, created in Christ Jesus for good works, which God prepared beforehand, that we should walk in them."* Why is this my favorite verse to demonstrate His creativity? The Greek word for "workmanship" is *poiēma* and is the word from which we derive poem and poetry. Paul is telling us in Christ we are God's great masterpiece. We are a work of art. We see ourselves so different from how He sees us. We see ourselves broken, as dirty rags. He says, "You are My beautiful masterpiece." God created, because His nature is to create. He is the Master Artist in every genre of creativity.

I am a huge *Lord of the Rings* fan. J.R.R. Tolkien, the author, was a brilliant storyteller. His books tell the story of a world from creation through several thousands of years. He created several cultures, with their own languages, history, poetry and songs, heroes and villains. It is considered by many to be the greatest work of storytelling ever written. Yet it has nothing over God's story found in the Bible. When we begin to understand the message and history of Scripture, it is more awesome, fantastic, and powerful than any other book ever written. Most don't see it because they have only looked at one part, the Fall of Man and the Cross. All they see is the salvation story. That seems to cover all that is needed. But that isn't true. Yes, the Cross, and most importantly Jesus Christ, is central to the story. Christ is the glue who holds it all together. Nevertheless, I believe Jesus would also say there is more for us; and I would propose that the end of our Bible is not the end of His story, or ours.

The nature of love is to create. I have a saying I share when I travel, particularly when I teach on identity: "Love must multiply." A man and woman fall in love and are married. Generally, at some point in time they desire to have children. The nature of love is to increase. My wife and I couldn't have children. There was a void in our hearts as we both always wanted children. When Patti was miraculously healed and became pregnant with our oldest son, Jason, we had so much joy. When Jay was born, we were both overwhelmed with love for this little guy. I didn't think my heart could contain more love. I felt more alive and purpose-driven than ever before.

Then our second son, Matthew, arrived. This might sound silly, but I was concerned because my love was so overwhelming for Jay, how could I possibly love Matt, too? But I did, and do, love him every bit as much as Jay, and he, too, brought life into our home through his unique personality. How does it work? When love is authentic, no strings attached, unconditionally given, our capacity to love is limitless. When we love this way, we become the image bearers we were created to be.

As Jesus followers, when we love this way His life rises up in us, His life-giving grace and our capacity to love increases. When our love becomes conditional, the life-giving power of Holy Spirit that empowers us to love is quenched. His love releases His power for life in our inner self. Again, you cannot separate His love from His life.

In His own counsel, the Godhead purposed and planned to create this universe and establish on a small planet the dwelling place, cosmic tabernacle, of the Lord. There was a determination made to create a species of beings that would be unique in that they would carry His presence, both now and forever.

However, the point was not to create empty vessels, but living beings with freewill, that they might choose to love Him. In this love, between Creator and His offspring, something about Him would be revealed, capturing both His heart, love, wisdom, character, and glory, putting Himself on display in ways His creation, in all its dimensions, could not see before.

> *To bring to light for everyone what is the plan of the mystery hidden for ages in God, who created all things, so that through the church* [ecclesia, the

called out ones to govern and serve] *the mani-fold wisdom of God might now be made known to the rulers and authorities in the heavenly places. This was according to the eternal purpose that he has realized in Christ Jesus our Lord* (Ephesians 3:9-11).

Here in Ephesians 3, the apostle Paul is telling us that God intended to make a mystery about Himself known to angelic beings, *rulers and authorities in the heavenly places,* through His children. Most importantly, through His relationship with us. The Greek word *ecclesia* or *ekklesia* is translated here as "Church." In Greek culture, the people identified as *ecclesia,* were citizens who, for a season, stepped out of their normal life to govern and serve both the government and the people. Who are those Paul is pointing toward in this context? Every believer is called to govern and serve as citizens of God's Kingdom.

We are to extend the influence of the government, culture, and power of His Kingdom. We do this by prayer, worship, preaching the truth, living out our faith, signs, wonders, and deliverance. Also, and perhaps most important, by being true lovers of God and people. It is amazing that in His plan He is revealing something of His power, glory, wisdom, and love to His creation, and it is best seen through His love for us and the power of His love to move the hearts of sinful humankind toward Him. Who loves that way? Only our God and Father.

If we look to the next section of Paul's letter to the Ephesians, we get a glimpse into what he believes, at least in part, is this mystery:

> *For this reason* **I bow my knees before the Father,** *from whom every family in heaven and on earth is named, that according to the riches of his glory he may grant you to be strengthened with power through his Spirit in your inner being, so* **that Christ may dwell in your hearts through faith**–*that you,* **being rooted and grounded in love, may have strength to comprehend with all the saints what is the breadth and length and height and depth, and to know the love of Christ that surpasses knowledge,** *that* **you may be filled with all the fullness of God** (Ephesians 3:14-19).

Paul here shifts our attention from government to family. He says this is the reason he bows and prays to our sovereign King and heavenly Father. His prayer is for us to become the people who reveal the mystery, a mystery rooted and grounded in love. When Paul refers to the *breadth and length and height and depth,* he is speaking into the four dimensions of our understanding of existence. This reflects back to Acts 17:28: *"In him we live and move and have our being."* This is where Paul is telling the Athenians gathered, His God fills space and time, therefore He is always present. The mystery, at least in part, is that the government of Heaven will be the family of God. A family firmly rooted and established by His love and in His love, to the point we will all together be filled to the fullness of Christ.

Consider the following Scripture phrase in Revelation regarding the idea that His government is exercised through His Son, and us, His brothers and sisters. Revelation 1:6 and 5:10 in most translations say, *"made us a **kingdom, priests** to his **God** and **Father,"*** Now what is interesting about these two verses is that some Bible translations cite "kings" instead of "kingdoms." The difference is which group of ancient manuscripts were used to interpret the text. The point is this, both are relevant. We are a kingdom of priests. And we are kings, lowercase k, to Jesus the High King, uppercase K. This speaks into our eternal role to govern on our Father's behalf with Jesus the only High King and Lord of all.

In my next book, *The Government Will Be on His Shoulders,* I will unwrap this more fully, but let it suffice for now, at least part of this mystery is the revelation of God as Father and His image bearers governing through the fullness of love we see in Christ. This is a work of the Spirit of God alone, through His indwelling presence and Life.

For us to carry the glory He desires to reveal about Himself through His people, freewill isn't only an option, but is in truth the only option. To create beings, put them on display as loving you, though they are powerless to do anything but show love and serve, is not glorious, any bully tyrant can do that. But to create beings with the freedom to choose or not choose to love you, to pursue them tenaciously in your love, not violating their freedom, then come in the flesh to reveal yourself as a lover so devoted you would die for them rather than be controlling, allowing them to freely fall in love with you or not, then once they freely yield to love, you transform them into your beautiful image as sons and daughters—*that* is glorious beyond expression.

This is an exquisite revelation of what makes Him glorious. What a revelation of the multifaceted beauty, splendor, and majesty of the only God who is pure love hidden for ages past. This is why we will forever be free in His love.

God's Dance—the Beauty of His Romance

I was raised in a Latin family who loved, and I do mean loved, to dance. My mom and dad, her five siblings and their spouses all loved to dance. If there was dance music on, they'd be dancing. As a result, I, all my siblings, and most of my cousins danced. There were twenty-one cousins within six families, and when we were all together, there was dancing.

I was in my late teens when the dance craze called The Hustle broke out. One summer I was dancing in contests around the New York area for extra money. I found that to dance well, at that level, I had to have a partner I could flow with. The more effortlessly I could lead the partner to respond to my movements, the easier it was to move fluidly together in unison; as one. Patti and I have been dancing together for many years now. We have a rhythm and a sensitivity in movement together. She knows my movements and I know hers, there is no thinking involved, we just dance. When two people can move that way, it is a beautiful thing to see.

Moving with the Lord in the Spirit this way is amazing, too. I believe when Jesus says, *"I only do what the Father is doing,"* carries the same type of sensitivity to the movements of God in the Spirit. The correlation is simple; as we become sensitive to Him, understanding His heart, how He moves and flows in certain situations, we begin to naturally supernaturally, almost instinctively, know what He is doing. It all flows from intimate connection, love, and adoration in our inner self.

We are created in the image of the Trinity. We are triune beings—body, soul, and spirit. We are three parts in one, not three separate stand-alone parts, but one integrated being. The body has it's function, as does the soul and the spirit. The Holy Spirit in union with our spirit is moving to bring us in balance, so we might function as God intended—with Holy Spirit in perfect union with our spirits. Our spirit is not the problem, our soul is. The place of our passions, desires, imagination, will, and thought life are the soul. God intends for the rudder of our ship to be the spirit, not the soul. Our soul is like a big-footed clumsy oaf with two left feet. It's not pretty to watch that guy dance, or even walk for that matter.

When the Spirit of God moves with our spirits, freewill begins to take authority over the soul. Slowly over time that big-footed beast tripping over everything, and making a big mess of our lives, starts to be transformed into the prince or princess we were made to be. When this happens, or better yet, *as* it happens, the three—body, soul, and spirit—work together in perfect unity as God intended. Suddenly we are sensitive to the One our soul loves. As His life in us rises, we begin to dance in unison, resonating and revealing the God who is love. We begin to love others rightly. Our entire self begins to live in wholeness.

> *For those who are led by the Spirit of God are the children of God* (Romans 8:14 NIV).

When a couple dances, the male leads, the female follows. If you have ever watched skilled dancers, generally all eyes are on the lady. She makes all the spins, jumps, etc. Every now and then, in a good team, the man will shine, but his role is different. If the man is not smooth, fluid, and gentle but firm in leading, it doesn't matter how great the woman is, the dance will fall apart. Equally, if the woman can't be led or resists in order to take the lead, the dance will be awkward and potentially dangerous. Moving with God is very much like this. When we are led by the Spirit, beautiful, wonderful, and powerful things happen. When we take the lead back and forth, the interaction is never what it could have been.

For the dance to be all it can be, the woman has to trust her male partner. In fact, if a couple has learned how to trust each other, they can even improvise, because of the trust. It is only by building trust and surrendering yourself to Holy Spirit that faith moves into power. Only through trust, faith, and passion for Him will you ever be able to do what He is doing. As you submit to His lead, His passion becomes yours.

I heard once that the beauty of dance isn't simply the movement of the dancers—the individual moves performed in unison—it is also the way the space between them is used and impacts what is seen. The times the dancers draw near and embrace, along with the space created in the separations. How the two fill and use the whole space they dance in is part of the beauty. The rhythm of the music dictates the dancers' movements—the way the music ebbs and flows, with crescendos and decrescendos. The syncopated rhythms require the dancers to work together. It isn't just what the people see, it is also what they hear and feel between the music and the dance. If done well, the dance moves the audience to be engaged and to become part of the dance. The dance becomes a shared experience.

The Lord, too, loves to dance. Kevin Prosch's song "Lord of the Dance" has the following lyrics: "You're Lord of the dance, You're the dancing Lord." We are invited into this dance of God, built on intimacy, surrender, trust, passion, and faith. The dance we are called into is immersed in love. Not just any love, it's the love of a Father for His children, who happen to also be the bride of His beloved Son. In His mystery we have been created to be the objects of His Son's desire. We are learning how to dance and move with Him, so we may reveal Him to the world. This can only happen by the working of the Spirit in us. Let's learn to dance with Him.

He Is Forever the Father and Bridegroom in Sovereignty

Marriage is the most beautiful and powerful gift we have from God in this natural world, when both people are mutually submitted, or perhaps better said, *committed,* to one another. Marriage is, in part, meant to be a window into the heart of what God wants our relationship with Him to be. Men being the head of the house is not a big deal if we love the way Jesus loves. When I look at Jesus, God incarnate, I see a lover and servant first, then Lord. Jesus never commanded His disciples to call Him "Lord." They called Him Lord because of what they saw Him to be. His compassion, wisdom, love, and, yes, His signs, too.

But Jesus never demanded them to call Him "Lord." He simply let the light of His love and the life it brings speak for Him. They saw Him as Lord, the sovereign King, because of the way He loved and He lived. His sovereignty is not built on Him being controlling. He doesn't need to control people in order to bring His purposes to fruition. Especially when you understand His core purpose is to have a people, a family, a citizenry in a Kingdom rooted and established in His love.

He is building His house with living stones, vessels carrying His presence. Yes, He could make anyone be obedient and cause us to surrender. He can easily decide, "I am choosing this one or that one, and I will use up the rest as tools to teach my chosen lessons." Is that perfect love in action? Is that the love that casts out fear? No. So what is the answer? We need to know how to take hold of Him and understand His good, pleasing, and perfect will.

> *Therefore, I urge you, brothers and sisters, in view of God's mercy, to* **offer your bodies as a living sacrifice**, *holy and pleasing to God—***this is your true and proper worship. Do not conform** *to the pattern of this world but* **be transformed by the renewing of your mind.** *Then you will be able to* **test and approve what God's will is—***his good, pleasing and perfect will* (Romans 12:1-2 NIV).

Romans 12:1-2 are among my favorite verses in the Bible. There is so much wisdom in them. When Paul says to *"offer your bodies as a living sacrifice,"* he isn't meaning to imply simply the action of your body, as in sexual immorality, he is saying we need to offer our whole self as a living sacrifice. You do understand your body simply does what your soul desires it to do. If you lust in your heart, your body responds accordingly.

Paul then tells us, *"this is your true and proper worship."* What is worship? The word *worship* came from the old English word *worth-ship*. So, worship is about the worth, or high esteem of something you value. We all worship something, it is unavoidable. God created us for worship, so we must worship something or someone. When we chose to rebel against God, we made a choice to worship ourselves. We had an insufficient understanding of the great value, treasure, God is. We also made a choice, unknowingly, to feed our own souls. We were made for both union with Him in our spirit, but also for Him to be the Source of life, Bread of Life, to our soul.

Our soul is fed by what we worship. Worship—I am not talking about singing songs, as important as that may be—is the core value of our soul, what we build our life on.

In Chapter 2, I shared that what you fix your eyes on will be your source of life. Your soul will feed on it and get life from it. In a codependent relationship, we try to get our soul needs through the other person. Since what we fix our eyes on is what we live for, we demand that person to meet our needs. What a recipe for disaster.

In contrast, when we offer all of ourselves as a sacrifice to God, we receive in return grace, Spirit life, in our souls. When we lay our own way on the altar of Christ, we give Him the greatest act of worship. Why? Because we have chosen to give Him what we could not in the Garden, our whole life, with all our self-centered desires. We are saying, "I love and desire You above all other lovers. You are my greatest love; I lay all others down." That is the romance of the Trinity we are invited into through the Cross, resurrection, ·

217

indwelling of Holy Spirit; to accept His unrelenting, wholly devoted love as Father, Bridegroom, and Lord.

The battle is between the life of God in you and the life of your soul. Your soul has had its own way for too long. The life of the Spirit is true life. The soul always leads us to conform to the world. It wants its own way; and the way to appease our spiritual desires is to take on the form of religion, mixing grace with performance. Or the soul can conform to the moral ideology of the world we live. We are living in a time when ideologies of the world are clashing with the reality of His Kingdom. If there ever was a time for the people of God to die to self, to vain philosophies, religion, worldly power and fame and embrace the transformation of the Spirit, today is that day.

When Paul says in Romans 12:2 to be transformed, we need to know what it means. Most people think we are becoming better people, better Christians from the inside out. The word *transforms* here in the Greek is the root word from where we get metamorphosis.

Metamorphosis is not the changing of a caterpillar into a butterfly. It is the complete undoing; nothing is left of the caterpillar. The caterpillar is not mostly dead—it is dead, dead, dead. Paul is saying let yourself, your soul, completely die to its own way. Take on the Spirit and kill your old self with all of its passions. This is an *all-in* commitment to Jesus. He died for us, now we die for Him. He came back to life; we will rise as a new creation through the same life.

For this to happen, we must have the right to say yes or no, He wouldn't have it any other way. His sovereign will, His providential purpose, is a Kingdom of wholehearted lovers. If you want to know His will, surrender everything to His love. Let His light reveal the dark places in you, then choose to give those things to Him and you will receive grace—life. The process is where you will begin to see His goodness more fully. You will begin to see what truly pleases Him. You'll discover what pleases Him is what brings you the greatest joy, peace, and passion.

The Beauty of It All

He is sovereign, the King is on His throne. Freewill doesn't change that reality. When we understand that fore-knowing, or foreseeing, and His predetermined choice is working together in partnership, it is easy to see the beauty of the both/and of freewill and God's sovereignty. We choose, He knows who will choose, not because He made them choose, but because He saw them choose. At just the right time He enters in and places the seal, the Holy Spirit. We work in harmony just like the dancers. In this synchro-nistic movement of hearts, He is glorified in and through us as we rejoice in Him, and He in turn rejoices, singing over us His great love for all creation. His beautiful children, bought with His blood, forever His bride in the unity of perfect love.

And all creation rejoices and praises Him as we are received into our eternal home.

I will wrap it all up with the following two testimonies as object lessons on freewill and sovereignty.

God's Sovereignty—An Object Lesson

In June 1986, I was driving home from a friend's church. I was invited to speak to their youth group. It was a great morning; I shared the Gospel and all but one of the thirteen or fourteen teens there gave their lives to the Lord. It was a perfect summer afternoon. The sun was brilliant, warm but not overly hot. The sky was completely clear as I drove up Wellwood Avenue.

As I was driving, I noticed an elderly man laid out on the ground on the side of the road. Next to him was a woman on her knees. I thought it was a strange sight, so I pulled over to see if I could help. When I reached them, I asked, "What happened? Is there anything I can do?" The woman calmly with conviction said, "He's dead."

My first thought was, *How would you know.* So I asked, "How do you know?"

"I'm an ER nurse at Good Samaritan Hospital. I was on my way home when I saw him collapse. I pulled over and got to him as fast as I could. I took his pulse, there is nothing and he has no breath sounds. He's dead."

I figured if anyone would know, an ER nurse would. Not knowing what else to do, I said, "I'm a Christian." As it turned out she was, too. I said, "I am going to pray." She agreed and bowed her head.

It was at least five or six minutes between her finding him and us praying; he was dead the entire time. I didn't really think much, I simply placed my hand on his chest and said, "In Jesus' name, come back." Immediately his chest rose. She checked his pulse and it was back. Not very strong, but steady. The ambulance came a couple of minutes later. We gave them some basic info, our names, addresses, and how we found him.

Later that week, the pastor of the Methodist church I was at that Sunday called me. He had a letter from the family. The man indeed had come back to life. The letter told us tests showed he had a massive heart attack and he should have died. Evidently, he had a long history of heart issues. They wanted the ER nurse (a woman I didn't know and never saw again) and I to know that their dad passed away later that night. They said, "Thank you, had you not done what you did, he would have died there. But instead, all of his family was with him. We all got to say goodbye. The opportunity to do that comforts us and we're thankful."

I did nothing but be obedient and take a small risk. The sovereignty of God stepped in and gave life, and with it a great kindness to the man's family.

Our Freewill—An Object Lesson

That same summer in 1986, I started meeting weekly with an elderly gentleman, my cousin's father-in-law, Joe. I'd known him since I was ten years old. He scared me. He seemed like a tough guy and I didn't know how to relate to him. Over the years when I'd see him, I was very respectful but kept my distance. His wife, Grace, however, gave her life to Jesus through a charismatic Catholic church, and unbeknownst to me, always liked me and had prayed for years for me. When she found out that I believed in Jesus, she was incredibly excited. And when she found I was a charismatic believer, she was over the moon.

I had a great fondness for Grace over the years. She was very religious in many ways, but she was so beautifully in love with Jesus. When her other daughter-in-law was stricken with cancer and only had a few days to live, Patti and I went to the hospital with Grace. We prayed for her and her eyes went from yellow to pure white, and her skin went from grey to a perfect healthy skin tone, so we had built a trust with Grace. About a year before this story began, Joe broke his back while at work in the garment district in New York City. It took him close to a year, I think, to get back on his feet.

That year humbled Joe and opened him up to hear about Jesus. But not from Grace, oh no, not her. So, Grace invited me for lunch one Wednesday. I don't like fish, but I do love tuna fish sandwiches. So, every Wednesday for three months or so, maybe more, at noon, Joe and I sat down, had tuna fish sandwiches and went through the Bible. This was one of the best things I ever did. Joe gave his life to Jesus. I watched tears roll down his cheeks over those months as he would repent for past sins and encounter God's love. Grace watched with tears in her eyes as her husband was transformed. Those times with him and Grace are like precious gems to me. After that season, life got busy and my times with Joe became less and less frequent.

About a year and a half passed by when my cousin called me. Joe was in the hospital and he wasn't going to make it. She told me he was asking for me. By the time I got to the hospital, about an hour had passed. Though I drove as fast as I could, he had slipped into a pre-death coma right after my cousin called me. I walked into the room and saw that Grace was there. My cousin was there with her husband, whom I knew well. They were obviously distraught as they told me it would be any time now. I asked how long they were at his bedside; it was a very long time. I suggested they take a break and grab a bite to eat; I would sit with him.

I waited a few minutes for them to leave the room. When I was sure they were a safe distance away, I pulled the curtain so no one could see. I stood next to Joe, who was completely in a comatose state, motionless, and said quietly but firmly, "Joe, come back, wake up in Jesus' name." Immediately, his head lifted up fully from the pillow, like he was going to rise up. He looked straight at me, shook his head "no" hard and fast, straightened out, and laid back down in a coma. I stood there stunned. After a few moments I said, "Okay, Joe. I love you."

I believe that in that moment, Joe was back—but he chose to stay with Jesus. He had the choice, freewill, to stay with us or be with the Lord. He chose the Lord. I learned that day, particularly around resurrection prayers, sometimes it is God's will to send them back or not. Sometimes the person has the freedom to choose. It isn't either-or. It isn't a cookie-cutter, one-size-fits-all Christianity. Our role is to pray in faith, that's all we can do. I fully expect to see resurrections. I also understand I carry but one part of the equation—obedience to pray. It's a walk in the midst of mystery. The dance of moving with the Spirit of Life in partnership, sovereignty here, freewill there, all of it in the gift, grace, that is the Spirit of God, our Comforter, Counselor, Teacher, Guide, and Guardian. He is the Joy we have been given and given abundantly.

God's sovereign hand can step in at any moment to do what only He can do. Our freewill doesn't diminish His sovereignty. Our freewill is a gift He gives from His sovereignty.

A Final Word

In closing, I hope that in reading this book there has been in some measure a shift in your personal theology regarding grace, how grace works—and most importantly, who God is in you and how much He loves you. I believe there is power in understanding grace as the very life of God working in you. It is so much more intimate and powerful than the view of a gift you don't deserve.

I hope you also received impartation to go and search out for yourself the truth and the heart of the Father. Paul prayed for God to deliver him from a thorn in his side, and God responded, *"My grace is sufficient."* The life of the Spirit was sufficient for Paul to overcome. The life of the Spirit was enough to strengthen him, keep him through many dangers, and, in the end, the grace that is Holy Spirit in us, was enough to bring him before the Lord he so loved.

The Spirit of Life in you is able to do the same for you, and so much more than you can possibly imagine. You can't be any closer to the One who loves you—after all, He is living in you, loving you from the inside out. What could possibly be better? Let Him shift your vision, your worldview, upward and fix your eyes on Him. Just wait and watch what He does in your life.

Go, heal the sick, raise the dead and almost dead, cast out demons, feed the poor, love the heartbroken, care for the afflicted, preach the Gospel in love, preach it by the life of His Holy Spirit who dwells in you. You can do all things through Christ who lives in you. Cheering you on as you transform the world you live in.

The Lord bless you and keep you; the Lord make his face shine on you and be gracious to you; the Lord turn his face toward you and give you peace (Numbers 6:24-26 **NIV**).

The Parable of the Wise Dolphin

IT WAS A BEAUTIFUL SPRING DAY when Zoe came bursting through the door at Grandpa's house. "Grandpa, Grandpa" she shouted. She was obviously upset as she just rambled on talking to someone who wasn't there, until she found Grandpa Jack in the family room.

"Hello, Zoe," Grandpa Jack said. "What are you so upset about?"

"Well, Grandpa, I heard something in Sunday school I don't understand, and I don't know what do to about it." Zoe was a bright, lively, and very curious 7-year-old who always had big questions. All she had to do was come in the room and she lit up her grandpa's world.

"Okay, okay calm down, Zoe," Grandpa lovingly said. "Tell me what is upsetting you."

"Grandpa, my Sunday school teacher, Ms. Patti, said, 'God is all around us and we can't live without Him, and He gives us life because He loves us.' But I can't see Him anywhere and I've never heard Him, so I don't understand. And I want to go to Heaven, so I think I have to know where He is and how I can find Him. But I don't know where to start, and then if I found Him, what would I say?"

Grandpa with a little chuckle said, "Okay, I get it Zoe. Come sit next to me. I want to tell you a story." Zoe jumped right up on Grandpa's lap and put her arm around him and said, "Okay, Grandpa, I'm listening."

"Zoe, once there was a fish named Thomas. He was a young fish, very lovable and kind, but also very gullible. He trusted everybody, which you know is not always a good thing. One day a very mean barracuda came and played a trick on Thomas. He said, 'Thomas, come here, I have very alarming news to share with you—very, very alarming news. I just found out that you have to find water, if you don't find water you won't be able to live.'

"Having said what he said, the mean barracuda left, laughing quietly in a sinister way, quite proud of himself for getting Thomas worked up and searching for water.

"Thomas frantically searched everywhere for water. In the distance he saw Mr. Crabb. Mr. Crabb was not the friendliest crab in the ocean, everyone called him crabby Mr. Crabb, but Thomas didn't care, he had to find water to live, and he had to find it soon, so he swam up to Mr. Crabb and said, 'Mr. Crabb can you help me?'

"Mr. Crabb said, 'I don't have time for any of your silliness, Thomas, leave me alone.'

"But Thomas was persistent. He said, 'Mr. Crabb, Mr. Crabb, you have to help me. I need to find water. Do you know where I can find some?'

"Mr. Crabb took one of his claws and just waved Thomas off saying, 'I have no time for your silliness. Go away, Thomas, stop wasting my time.' And he was gone.

"This upset the little fish even more and he became more frantic, worrying what would happen if he didn't find water soon.

"Thomas could see a little ways from him a bunch of tunas swimming. He thought, *Surely with that many tuna fish swimming together someone must know where I can find water.* So, Thomas swam up and shouted, 'Wait! Do you know where I can find water? If I don't find water soon I will die!' But they all just laughed at him and swam away.

"Mr. Dolphin, who had been watching Thomas all along, swam over to him and said, 'Thomas, I've been watching you frantically swimming all around. It looks like you're searching for something. What is it you're looking for?' Mr. Dolphin was very nice, he had a reputation for being very wise and kind; and although Thomas was made fun of before, he knew Mr. Dolphin would help.

"'Well, Mr. Dolphin,' Thomas said, 'Mr. Barracuda told me that he was very alarmed and that I would die if I didn't find water. I was swimming everywhere asking everybody where I could find water, so I won't die. But everybody just laughed at me or said mean things to me. Nobody will answer me.'

"'I understand, Thomas,' said Mr. Dolphin. 'First let me say you should not listen to Mr. Barracuda; he is not to be trusted and he likes to play games with youngsters like you.'

"Thomas answered, "Okay sir, I will not listen to him anymore. But could you tell me where I can find water. I don't want to die.'

"'Thomas, you're not going to die. You live in water. When you swim, you're swimming in water. When you eat, you eat in water. When you play, you're in water. Even when you sleep, you sleep in water. The ocean you live in is all water…in water you live, and you move, and you are who you are. Water is life for you, and it provides all that you need. In fact, we that live in the ocean consider it to be like a father to us, providing everything we need to live.'

"'So, Mr. Dolphin sir, are you saying that I was already in water and I have always been in water, though I didn't know it? And that it has always been giving what I need, even though I didn't know that either?'

"'Yes, Thomas, that is what I am saying. You are in the water, and the water is in you, as you breathe water in and out. You are immersed in it, always have been and always will be. There is nothing to worry about.'

"The end," said Grandpa.

Zoe looked at Grandpa and said, "Grandpa, that's a very nice story…but I don't understand how it answers my question about not seeing or hearing God."

"Well, Zoe, you are like Thomas who lived in the ocean, saturated in living water because he lived in the ocean and it gave him life."

"So, Grandpa, are you saying that God is like the ocean?"

"Well, yes in a way," Grandpa answered.

"You see, Zoe, God is all around us. He is in the air we breathe. He is in the beautiful things we see. He is everywhere. But unlike the ocean water, God is a Person and He is love. From His love we receive life. And He is light to help guide us through life, living in love and truth. So while the story gives us an idea of how God works, God is so much bigger and more beautiful."

"Ms. Patti said Jesus came from Father God and died so we could go to Father God and be friends again. Is that true?"

"Yes, it is. Jesus came to bring us back into friendship with the Father. Though we can't see the Father, for a little while we saw Jesus and we will be with Him again. We got to see and understand how good Papa God is. Because Jesus came to restore us, if we believe in Him, the Spirit of Father God lives in us, loving us and giving us life, teaching us and helping us grow wise.

"Like Thomas living in the ocean and receiving every good thing from it, we live immersed in the Father…and if we say yes to Jesus in our heart, as we live in Father God, we get His Spirit, Holy Spirit, living in us, giving us every good thing we need. So you need not worry. You don't have to look for Him. God is in every sunrise and sunset, in the beauty of the oceans and the mountains and the stars at night. He is even in the air we breathe."

"And even in me, Grandpa?"

"Yes, even in you, Zoe."

"Wow! He is a lot bigger than I thought He'd be."

"God is pretty cool, isn't He?"

"Yea, very cool. Are there any of GG's chocolate chip cookies in the kitchen? I'm hungry after all that talking."

"Ha! Me too! Let's go see what we can find. You want some milk to dunk them in?"

"You know I do...what better way to eat GG's cookies!"

About the Author

PHILL URENA is a pastor, teacher, author, coach, and conference speaker. He is the founder of Kingdom Convergence, a ministry devoted to empowering the saints to live from the reality of God's love and equipping the church to make Jesus known through His signs and wonders. Phill is married to his best friend, Patti. They have two sons, a beautiful daughter-in-law, and two grandchildren.

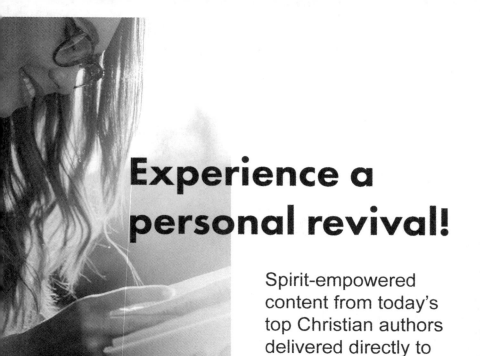

Experience a personal revival!

Spirit-empowered content from today's top Christian authors delivered directly to your inbox.

Join today!
lovetoreadclub.com

Inspiring Articles
Powerful Video Teaching
Resources for Revival

Get all of this and so much more, e-mailed to you twice weekly!

LOVE TO READ CLUB
by 𝕯 DESTINY IMAGE